RUNNING MY WAY

Harry Wilson

SACKVILLE BOOKS

First published in 1988
by Sackville Books Ltd
Stradbroke, Suffolk
England

Designed and produced by Sackville Design Group Ltd

Art Director: Al Rockall
Editor: Heather Thomas

British Library Cataloguing in Publication Data
Wilson, Harry,
Running my way.
1. Athletics. Running – Manuals
I. Title
796.4'26

ISBN 0-948615-07-0

Printed and bound in Great Britain by Hazell Watson & Viney

Contents

To the memory of the late
Sue Baxter who loved running
and gave it all she had.

HARRY WILSON

Harry Wilson started coaching in 1958 after a moderately successful career as an athlete (he represented his county, Hertfordshire, at all distances from 100m to marathon and ran for Wales in the World Cross-Country Championships).

He gradually made the transition from coaching sprinters to middle and long-distance runners. Since then he has coached more than 60 internationals of whom the most successful is Steve Ovett, Olympic champion and World Record Holder. Many of Harry's training routines, which have now become accepted worldwide, were pioneered in conjunction with Ovett.

Among the other international athletes he has coached are Johann Boakes, Julian Goater, Phil Norgate, Tony Simmons, Angela Tooby, Kirsty Wade and Josephine White.

Harry is the British National Event coach for 800m and 1500m and was coach to the British team at the last two Olympic Games and World Championships. He is a frequent lecturer and visiting coach at conferences and training camps all over the world, including Australia, Canada, Finland, France, Holland, Nigeria, the United States and Zambia.

He is the author of the biography *Running Dialogue,* part-author of the official IAAF and BAAB training manuals and several coaching books and a contributor to *The AAA Runner's Guide.*

TALBOT
8
TALBOT
6

Foreword by Steve Ovett

How good do you think I can be?

Why can't I run faster than him?

I train hard so why can't I win races?

How long is a piece of string?

Imagine being asked questions like these over and over again by different people all demanding absolute answers. It seems like a nightmare, but a coach's job is no different to this in its very essence.

Coaches have to deal most of their time with higher abstract qualities such as doubt, potential, despair, elation etc., as well as the basic animal feelings of fatigue, pain and fear. Their trade is not in absolutes; that is the property of the athlete – he or she either wins, loses, succeeds or fails.

So when an individual goes to a coach and asks to be helped with his training, he assumes, rightly or wrongly, that the person that he has asked has the intuitive capabilities to handle the task ahead.

It is very easy to coach on a grand scale with large numbers in the herd principle, where the training is geared to the average, and personal involvement is limited to group awareness, but the wastage in individual potential is enormous and success comes only for the few. So some coaches limit their numbers to groups that they feel they can justify, for they truly believe that to bring out the very best in any athlete they have to know the person as an individual, almost better than they know themselves.

Coaches have to take a truly objective view, weighing up such details as emotion, physical need and potential – factors that are not always obvious to the athlete. Noting these qualities or disabilities, they can then begin the difficult process of training and developing an individual as best they can.

Dealing in abstracts where individuals are concerned can be a volatile area, and more often than not, as with the alchemists of old, success is all too infrequent, whereas failures litter the ground.

I suppose I have painted this chasm of athletic paranoia because I, more than most, have come across the destructive type of coaching at all levels that has left me numb with disbelief at the flagrant waste of talent.

I was fortunate, some say fated, but it remains a simple fact that at the age of fifteen or so I met, or literally ran across, Harry Wilson.

What he saw in me at the time we are now all aware of in the athletic sense, but believe me it must have been pretty hard then to discern anything worth spending an enormous amount of time and effort on, as the talent was clouded with more than a few problems.

Harry, however, just seemed to clear all of these away as time went on and with just the basic instrumentation of coaching he not only developed my athletic talent to the full but also he allowed the mere training work-load itself to slowly mould and develop my character, and then finally to let it strengthen that character.

I was given training sessions that I thought were going to be easy. They were not. They were just about all I was capable of at the time, and then there were other sessions that on paper just looked impossible to achieve, but they were accomplished exactly as Harry said they would be.

What I am trying to express I suppose is that Harry Wilson is more than a coach in the same way that some athletes are more than just runners, jumpers or throwers. They rise above the norm by their innate ability to succeed where others for no apparent reason do not. They instinctively know when a thing is right.

Harry has over the period of many years coached tens, if not hundreds, of athletes of all ages and abilities. His love of watching people achieving the best from themselves is not just limited to the obvious medal tally, but in sharing with all his athletes those all too wonderfully brief moments in sport when an individual succeeds in doing better than his best.

This book then sets out to help athletes by presenting the basic principles of training and competition like many others before, but where it differs is that it is written by someone the Chess World would title a Grand Master. But in my view he is much more: a Merlin of the track. Experienced, wise, cunning and, when he turns base human elements into athletic gold, truly quite magical.

CHAPTER ONE

GETTING AHEAD

Running My Way will help you to develop a way of training and racing that will eventually become "your way".

The programme I recommend contains no magic formulas; the plans I advocate are not the only ones that may bring success; indeed I have never believed in the dogmatic types of training systems that preach the message "this is the only way – there is no other". I feel that several of the different methods that have been used to produce outstanding results may have owed their success more to the brilliance of a few practising athletes rather than to the basic soundness of the training programmes.

Although my approach is based on sound physiological principles, it has been developed mainly as a result of working for over 25 years with many runners of varying capabilities. You will not find many references to physiology text-books in the chapters that follow, but you will find many examples of training carried out by runners who have improved their own personal performances. I freely acknowledge that much of my knowledge of endurance training is based on:

1 My own personal experiences as a runner with a wide range of marks such as 200m-22.8sec, 800m-1min 58.6sec, 10,000m-30min 35sec and marathon 2hr 39 min.

2 The ideas and information gained through conversations with hundreds of runners, many of them world class.

3 Watching the effects of varying loads and mixtures of training on the athletes I have coached.

I have always felt that my role as a coach was to have athletes who, win or lose, came away from races able to say, "Well, I'm satisfied with that run." I know what it feels like after a satisfying performance – you ache, yet you feel good. You are self-satisfied, but not smug – and there is a voice inside you that wants to shout out, "Didn't I do well?"

I realise that in trying to achieve my objective, I have to try to fulfil the aspirations of a wide range of runners. Some of you will be happy to win a local event, others will aim to qualify for a National Championship and yet others will have an Olympic medal as their target. But the majority of you will feel satisfied each time that you run a bit faster than ever before, or finish in front of someone who has always previously beaten you.

Here I am putting a group of international runners through their paces on a typical training run on a hilly cross-country course in the woods

It is true that thousands of runners dream about winning Olympic medals but very few of them will go out and do what is necessary to make their dreams come true. Dreaming will not win medals; results will come from hard, progressive training and long-term intelligent planning.

Of course, there is no denying the fact that, to a considerable degree, the amount of success that you will eventually achieve will depend on the amount of natural talent that you possess, but this is not the only contributory factor. It is how you make the best use of what assets you do possess that counts – how you exploit your strengths, how you play down your deficiencies. I have known many runners who have possessed great natural physical ability, but who have never had the determination, discipline or intelligence to make the most of their assets. On the other hand, I have also known many runners who seemed to have all the odds stacked against them when it came to such physical factors as speed, strength and mobility, yet who have performed remarkably well due to their determination and 'stickability'. It is quite common to meet athletes who had great natural ability and who did extremely well when they were at school, but who failed to make their mark as seniors. "I was just as good as Bill Bloggs (the National Champion) when I was younger, but I never really got down to serious training – I guess he was just lucky." They do not seem to appreciate that Bill Bloggs' ability to train hard was not just a stroke of luck, but as vital a part of his athletic make-up as his natural physical ability.

My philosophy has been to get all the athletes I coach to appreciate that they have been fortunate enough to have been given some natural ability and to try to develop this talent to its utmost. To achieve this objective means recognising that it will take several years of sensible, dedicated training. I often use the phrase "It's not necessarily the best athlete who wins, but the best prepared." Certainly all the natural talent in the world will not help the runner who has lost his fitness due to lack of preparation.

You must not think that my "give it all you've got" approach means that there is nothing else in life apart from running. This is a dangerous attitude and one likely to lead to severe mental and physical distress. When you are doing your athletics make sure that it has all your concentration, but take care that you can switch off and put your mind to other things when your training is completed. To make yourself a good runner means that on most occasions your running will come first, but I would not like to think that it was contributing in any way towards the production of "athletics morons". Even those of you who are talented enough to make a career from your running must ensure that you do not work 24 hours a day, every day. No matter how you earn your living, it is vital that you allow adequate time for relaxation and recuperation, both mental and physical. Of course, some activities such as excessive drinking, smoking, drug-taking, insufficient sleep, etc. will negate your training efforts and will also lead to poor health. There is no way that an unhealthy body can handle the demands of hard training. However, I would hope that you are sensible enough to appreciate this point and to treat your body with respect. Get your priorities right – if it is important enough for you to train well each day, ensure that other activities do not prevent you from doing this.

What did I mean when I used the phrase 'natural physical ability'? What are the various factors that determine your ability to be a good endurance runner? In order to list these physical factors, I will need to describe briefly the physiological energy processes that occur when you run.

The physiology of running

The energy you need for running is derived from a chemical breakdown of glycogen, a substance stored in the muscles and liver. Unfortunately, as in most aspects of life, we do not get 'something for nothing' and the result of converting glycogen into energy is the production of a waste product – lactic acid. If you were to receive no outside assistance, you would quickly use up your glycogen reserves and be left with a build-up of lactic acid. However, by extracting oxygen from the air you breathe in, you initiate another chemical process whereby the lactic acid plus oxygen reconverts to glycogen; so if you run easily and have a good oxygen intake you can continue running almost indefinitely. This is an *aerobic* (with oxygen) activity and is the energy process used by marathon runners.

However, there are some explosive activities that are of such short duration that they are completed before oxygen intake has had time to take effect (eg. 100m), or are so intense that oxygen intake is insufficient to eliminate the lactic acid that is formed, and these are known as *anaerobic* (without oxygen) activities. I have known 100m runners who take in a deep breath on the command 'set', exhale violently when the gun fires, and only breathe in again when the race is completed. There is a large build-up of lactic acid during 100m races and this is cleared away by a period of heavy breathing after the race. So you could call the 100 metres a 100 per cent anaerobic activity and the marathon virtually a 100 per cent aerobic activity.

Between these two extremes come the middle-

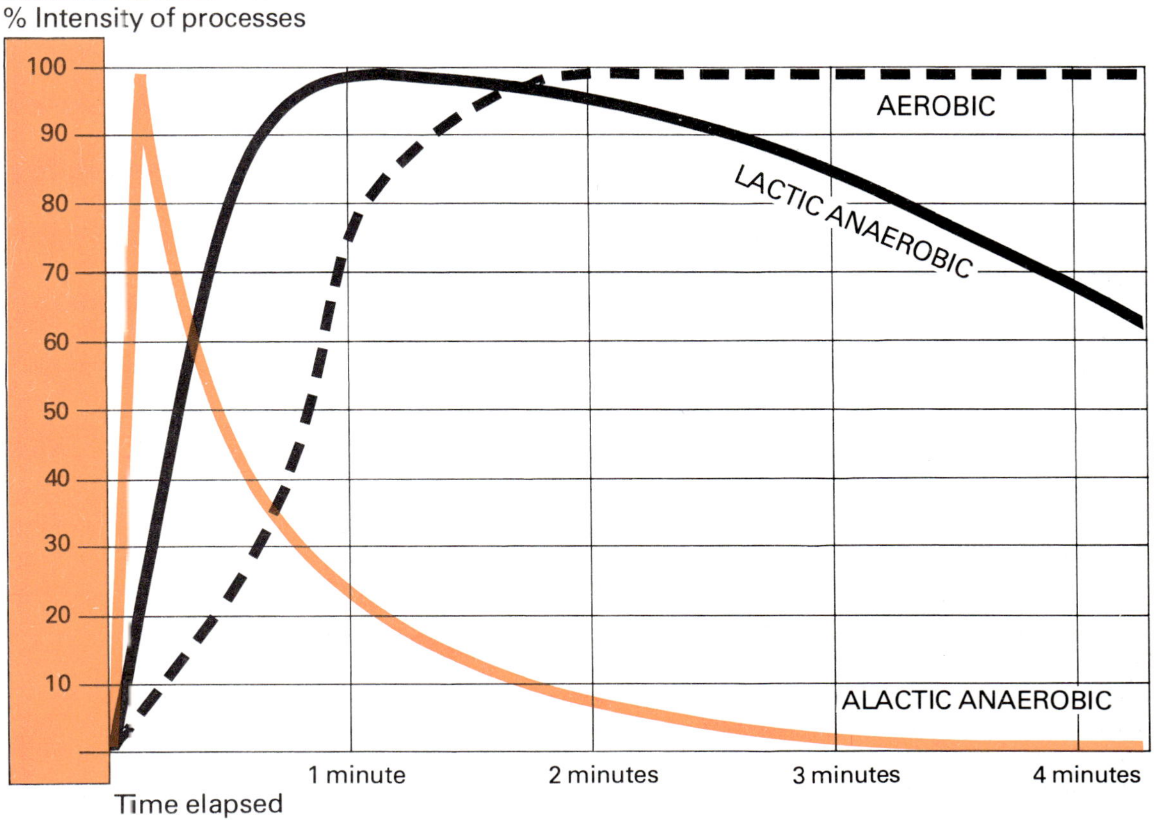

Graph 1: typical % utilization of each energy system when related to a class performance over 1 mile

distance events, in which you use both energy processes; ie. the pace of the race is so fast that the oxygen uptake cannot convert all the lactic acid to glycogen and there is a lactic acid debt built up which can only be cleared when the race is completed. Because the speed is greater in the shorter middle-distance races (800m/1500m), the anaerobic process will be utilized more than in the longer 5000m and 10,000m races, but it is important to appreciate that for much of the time during races both energy processes are working simultaneously. Some runners (and coaches) find it difficult to appreciate this and imagine that in an 800m race, the first part is run aerobically and then this process switches off and the anaerobic process is switched on for the later stages of the race. Do these people imagine that you stop breathing and taking up oxygen in the later stages? A study of the accompanying graph will help you to understand the utilization of the different energy systems.

Oxygen is picked up by the red cells in your blood and your blood is kept constantly circulated around your body by the pumping action of your heart. Fortunately your heart is not just the "Headquarters of Romance" as portrayed in romantic novels, but is the most vital and enduring of all your body's muscles – it never takes a day off. As you will see in Graph 1 there is a constant flow of oxygen enriched blood from your lungs to your working muscles and tired blood from the muscles back to your lungs, with your heart acting as the intermediate pumping station along the route. Your heart responds to your muscles' demands for refreshed blood by increasing its pumping rate and also its stroke/volume. This response means that you can measure the intensity of your training by counting your heart rate. The average person's heart rate while resting is approximately 72 beats per minute, so when you know that Steve Ovett's heart rate when he is resting is usually 36 beats per minute, then you

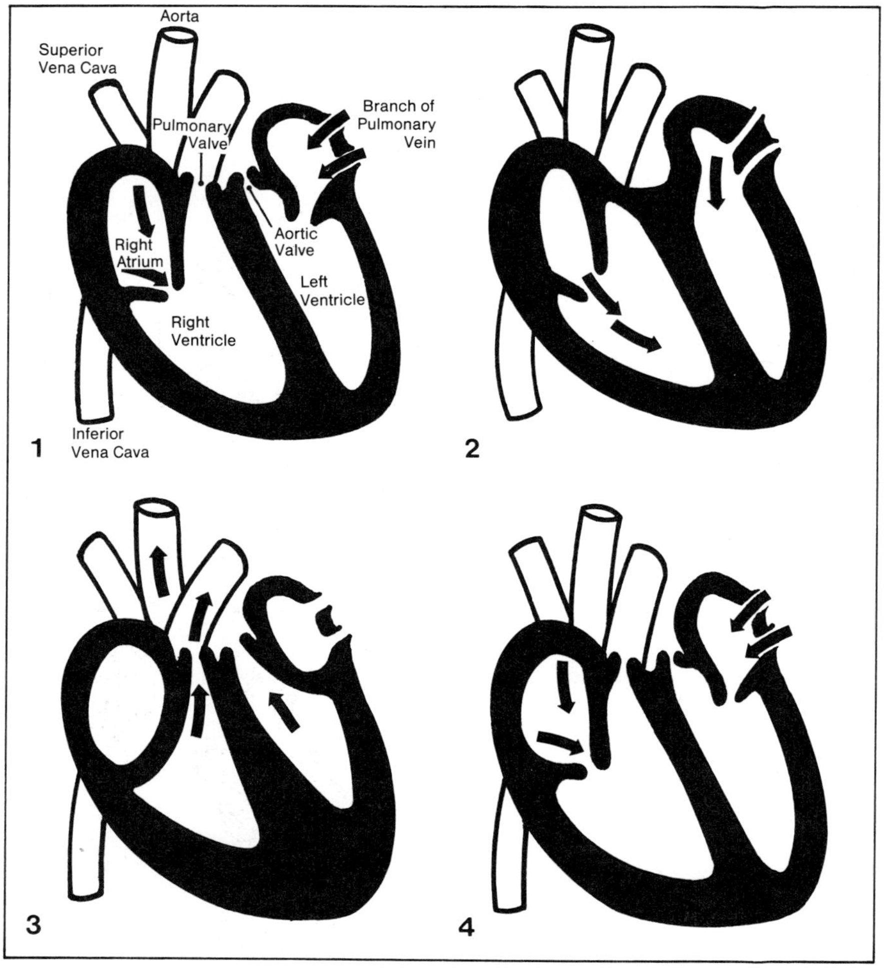

This series of diagrams shows the action of the heart in the body. **1** *Deoxygenated blood returns to the heart and enters the atria while the heart is relaxed between beats.* **2** *As the atria contract, the valves between the auricles and ventricles open and the blood passes into the ventricles.* **3** *The ventricles contract to pump the blood through the aorta valves into the pulmonary artery.* **4** *The blood is taken to the lungs to be oxygenated and the heart relaxes until the atria fill with blood again. The pulmonary veins return the oxygenated blood to the heart through the left ventricle and from there through the aorta to the rest of the body. This is a continuous cycle*

can appreciate that his heart is twice as efficient as the average person's. A powerful heart would no doubt have been one of Steve's natural assets, but its development to its present remarkable condition is the result of years of regular and progressive training.

Although the skeletal muscles depend on a constant flow of blood in order to do their work, the type of work that they are most capable of carrying out depends on their innate structure. Muscles are made up of millions of tiny fibres of which there are basically two types: the fast-twitch fibres that work quickly but not for very long; and the slow-twitch fibres which work more slowly but for longer periods. The balance of these two types of fibres basically determines the type of activity for which you are best suited, ie. if you are blessed with a preponderance of fast-twitch fibres, then you will be good at short duration, explosive events, but if you have many more

The male muscular and skeletal system ▶

1 Frontalis
2 Trapezius
3 Deltoid
4 Pectoralis major
5 Triceps brachii
6 Latissimus dorsi
7 Biceps brachii
8 Brachioradialis
9 Rectus abdominis
10 Pectineus
11 Rectus femoris
12 Vastus lateralis
13 Peroneus longus
14 Peroneus brevis
15 Tibialis anterior
16 Extensor digitorum longus
17 Sphenoid
18 Mandible
19 Hyoid bone
20 Cervical column
21 1st rib
22 Clavicle
23 Scapula
24 Sternum
25 Humerus
26 Costal cartilage
27 12th rib
28 Ulna
29 Sacrum
30 Radius
31 Pelvic inlet
32 Ischium
33 Pubis
34 Carpals
35 Metacarpals
36 Phalanges
37 Adductor longus
38 Gracilis
39 Sartorius
40 Femur
41 Vastus lateralis
42 Patella
43 Tibia
44 Soleus
45 Fibula
46 Tarsals
47 Metatarsals
48 Phalanges
49 Axis
50 Ilium
51 Coccyx
52 Adductor magnus
53 Semitendinosus
54 Sartorius
55 Trapezius
56 Supraspinatus
57 Deltoid
58 Infraspinatus
59 Teres minor
60 Teres major
61 Latissimus dorsi
62 Gluteus medius
63 Gluteus maximus
64 Iliotibial tract
65 Biceps femoris
66 Gastrocnemius
67 Soleus

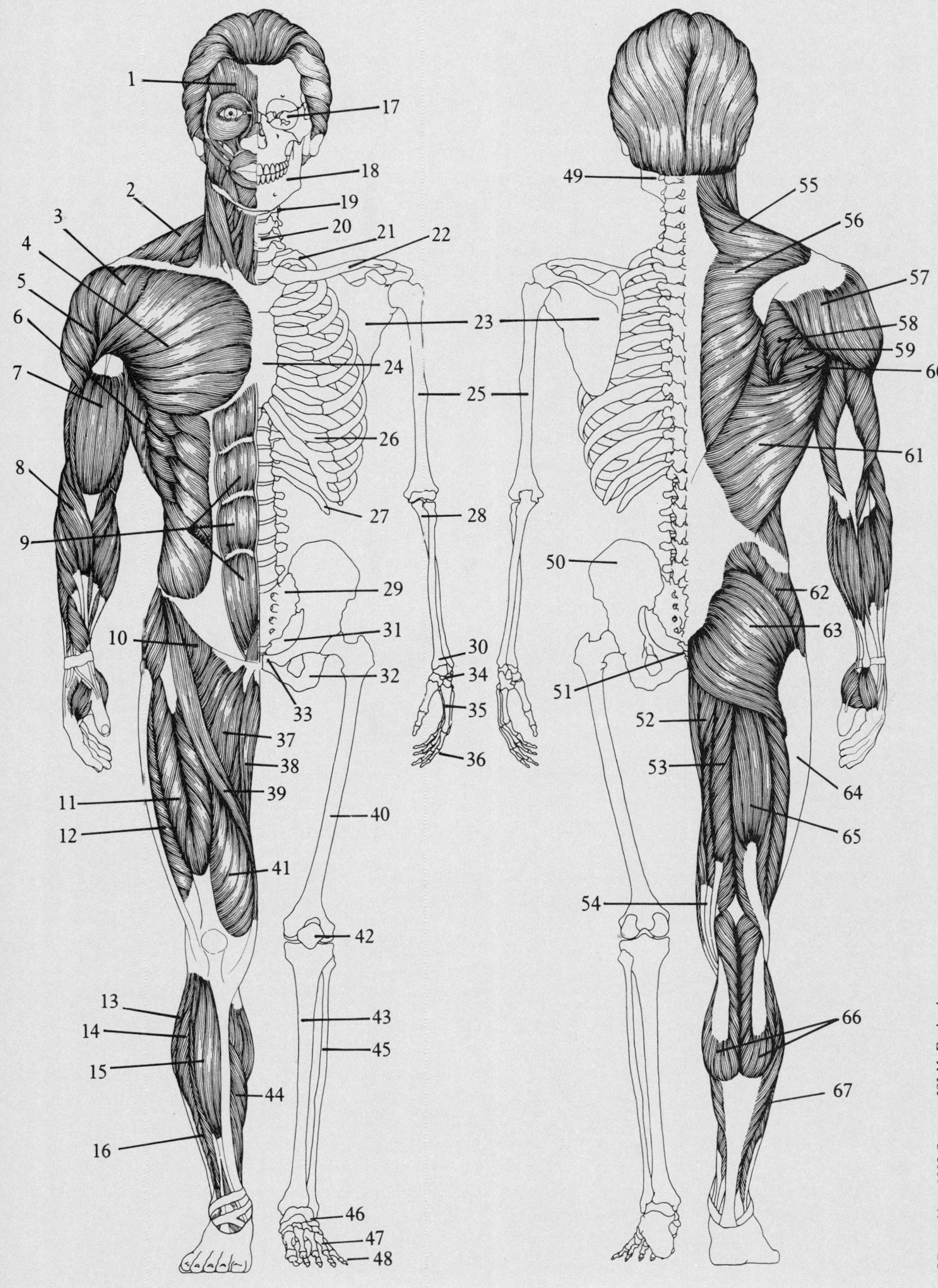
1
2
3
4
5
6
7
8
9
10
11
12
13
14
15
16
17
18
19
20
21
22
23
24
25
26
27
28
29
30
31
32
33
34
35
36
37
38
39
40
41
42
43
44
45
46
47
48
49
50
51
52
53
54
55
56
57
58
59
60
61
62
63
64
65
66
67

slow-twitch fibres then you will be better at the longer duration, endurance events. It does not take much imagination to appreciate that not only will top-class middle-distance runners have a roughly equal balance of slow- and fast-twitch fibres, but they will also have a larger overall volume of these fibres. The ratio between these fibres appears to be inherent and is not altered by training, but correct training improves the quality and efficiency of whatever muscle fibres you do possess. Although at the moment we are dependent upon the heart and muscle fibres that we have at birth, it is not impossible to visualize a time when the transplant industry is so efficient that athletes could be given different muscle fibres or a more powerful heart. Imagine being able to find the space within an athlete to give him the heart of an elephant – so strong that it needs to beat only 12 times a minute!

This short section on physiology is very basic, but I hope that it is sufficient for you to appreciate what happens within your body when you run. If you wish to explore this fascinating subject more fully, there are many excellent books on exercise physiology which you can buy or borrow from your local library, but remember that there are still areas for study that are not understood completely by the experts. I stress that the information I have given you is quite basic, but I also feel that it is important that you understand the basics as they are the foundation upon which any training programmes should be based.

So now you are in a position to consider the natural assets that an endurance runner should possess and to assess where training can bring about improvement.

Three basic rules

Athletics training is based on three sound physiological concepts:

1 Your body will adapt to gradual and progressive loads

Whenever you introduce a new or different activity, you should commence it at a level well within your capabilities, then gradually increase the load as your body adapts. Because we are all individual and not machines, we adapt at our own pace which explains why some runners respond much quicker than other runners to similar loads of training. If you are a young athlete, you must be prepared to wait several years before you start to realise your full potential. I can remember consoling Steve Ovett after a 1 mile race in Stockholm in 1974 when, at the age of 18 years he had run a remarkable 3min 58sec but had only finished seventh after being right up with the leaders at 1500m. "What's wrong, Harry? What do I need?" was Steve's protest. "All you need is time," was my reply. It was really another three years before Steve could handle a fast finish at the end of a hard-paced 1 mile or 1500m race. But in those three years he had covered several thousands of miles, completed hundreds of training sessions and gained experience in many good quality races. These benefits could not be gained in a few weeks or months, so it is a good lesson to you young athletes – be patient and allow your body to adapt gradually to the stresses of training.

2 Your body does not just adapt – it overcompensates

If you impose a training load upon yourself, your body not only adapts to handle that load, it overcompensates so that it can handle even heavier loads, if necessary. Your body's ability to overcompensate means that very rarely are you able to tap your physical resources to the full and it usually needs some extraordinary impetus to bring out the absolute best in yourself. I imagine that even Ben Johnson could sprint faster if he was being pursued by a hungry lion.

3 Your body needs time to adapt and recuperate

It is vital to allow adequate recovery time between training sessions and to plan for easy days or easy periods in your training plan. To train hard day after day may sound dedicated, but it does not make good sense and there are times when a day off may do you more good than another hard training session. To plan for recuperation periods is good thinking but must not be confused with opting out of training sessions because you do not feel like it or because the weather is bad.

We can now return to list the natural physical assets that are needed by the good endurance runner. Ideally, we are looking for someone who

Left: David Moorcroft was a late developer whose athletic success was a triumph of persistence
Above: Seb Coe, seen here beating Steve Cram, has the ideal build for a middle-distance runner

is naturally blessed with:

1 A light, well-proportioned frame that can adopt an efficient and economical running technique. Long legs, large feet, broad shoulders and chest, and narrow hips all contribute to an ideal physique as would a large range of movement in the limbs.
2 A powerful heart, efficient circulatory system and lungs capable of large expansion.
3 Skeletal muscles that possess a good quantity and a reasonable balance of the different muscle fibres, so that both speed and endurance are present in abundance.
4 An overall strong constitution that is not prone to illness and that can tolerate and adapt to intensive training.

Along with these physical factors, the ideal runner would also possess:

1 The determination to push his/her body on the right training and racing occasions for beyond the average limits of exhaustion. Endurance running is one of the few sports where the athlete has to suffer prolonged pain in training and racing in order to achieve satisfaction. I often hear teachers and coaches stressing to runners that they "must enjoy their sport". Do they really know what it is like to voluntarily subject the body to a series of fast repetitions in training without much recovery, or to maintain a blistering pace in a 10K cross-country race, regardless of the terrain or weather? Enjoying your sport is not really the appropriate phrase – gaining satisfaction or fulfilment is probably more apt. I have certainly never seen such great runners as Seb Coe, Steve Cram, Steve Ovett or David Moorcroft (all world record holders) whistling happy tunes during one of their history-making runs.

2 The patience to wait for results to come. David Moorcroft was 30 when he broke the World 5000m Record – 16 years after starting running; Carlos Lopes was 34 when he won the Olympic marathon in 1984; and there is a whole string of Russian and Rumanian women who have only reached

Above: Russian runner Tatiana Kazankina was a successful athlete although she suffered constantly from a mild form of anaemia

Below: the Brazilian Joachim Cruz won the 1984 Olympic 800m with one leg a little shorter than the other

world class in their late twenties or early thirties. Many of these athletes will have been competing for 15-16 years before reaching their full potential.

3 The belief that improvement can be made whatever the athlete's limitations. This conviction will have to carry an athlete through the periods that invariably come when performance appears to be at a standstill.

4 The discipline to develop a routine that enables the runner to live a reasonable life and fit in daily training. Developing a good routine is vital and many world class runners have told me that their really good results come when they have been able to maintain a planned routine for a long

period. Injuries, illness, family crises etc. all conspire to upset a routine, but a good athlete has to be prepared to expect such difficulties occasionally, face up to them sensibly and return to a routine as soon as possible.

5 The intelligence, native cunning, or whatever you care to call it, to appreciate what he/she is trying to achieve in training and to know when to crack the whip or when to ease up. A runner needs to be able to assess the factors that are needed to produce a performance in a particular race, to assess how he/she matches up to these requirements, then devise and carry out a training programme that will close the gap between these two assessments. Intelligence is also needed to race successfully and there is nothing worse than to watch a runner who has trained well proceed to race stupidly and produce a result that is nowhere near his/her potential.

Do not be worried if you feel that you fall a little short of the ideal characteristics I have described – join the club of 99.9 per cent of the world's runners. I doubt if there has ever been a perfect runner and in many instances some of the world's greatest have done well despite some of the odds being stacked against them. Joachim Cruz (1984 Olympic 800m Champion) has one leg about one inch shorter than the other; Tatiana Kazankina (the Russian 800m/1500m Olympic Champion) suffered constantly from mild anaemia; Murray Halberg (1960 Olympic 500m Champion) had a wasted arm following polio – there are many more examples that I could quote. You must accept the hand you have been dealt, and then develop it to its utmost and make the most of your potential.

Murray Halberg overcame the handicap of a wasted arm – the result of polio

Personal circumstances

Your ability to train properly depends to a large degree on your personal circumstances and there are several factors to consider when you plan your programme:

1 Time
Have you the time available to fit in the proposed training? You will probably start off by training no more than once a day and gradually build up to twice a day over a period of years. Once a day means allocating 30 to 90 minutes daily to your running, depending upon the nature of the session, and there should be no difficulty in finding this amount of time. Remember to allow at least 3-3½ hours after a meal before training and to try to have something to eat within 1-1½ hours of completing the session. The after-training meal should be light but nourishing containing carbohydrates, protein and minerals. If you do a manual job or are involved in energy consuming activities like housework, gardening or being a physical education student, try to have at least an hour's relaxation before tackling a training session. Some sessions such as a steady run, or fartlek, can be done by running directly from your home and take little time. A track session involves a journey to and from the track and you will need to allow extra time to allow your body to cool down after a hot shower. This reduces the risk of catching a cold – particularly in cold, damp weather.

Moving up to twice a day becomes much more difficult as you need to allow an adequate recovery time between the two sessions as well as the digestion time after meals. The most common practice nowadays is to run your easier session in the morning, say, between 7am and 9am, and have a light meal after the session. Have a further meal at 1pm – carry out the harder session between 5pm and 7pm and follow this with your evening meal. This plan enables you to do a normal day's work, or to go to school, and is a popular routine carried out by many runners. I know some runners who prefer to carry out the harder session first – two of the women I coach, Chris Benning and Kirsty Wade, are typical examples – but this usually means that they have sufficient time to train a little later – say between 10am and 11am. One athlete I coached, Steve Harris (1983 World Student Games 5000m Champion), did a full day's work and had the singular ability to do an intensive track session at 8.30am.

If you are unable to train during daylight hours, then darkness during the winter months may influence your choice of training – obviously you cannot run across the countryside in the dark. If this is the case, then you will have to plan to run over the country at weekends and to make sure that your track sessions coincide with the flood-lighting at your local track. Darkness and its accompanying hazards create a special worry to women runners and it may be that you have to

alter your schedule to run in your lunch hour. In any case, I recommend that women train on well-lit roads and if possible be accompanied by another runner. If you are a woman runner and cannot find a running companion, or someone to ride alongside you on a bicycle, then I recommend that you carry an aerosol can of spray paint – just in case. I stressed earlier the importance of developing a routine, which is why it is difficult to fit in your training if you have a job that involves a lot of travelling.

Left: Kirsty Wade completes a hard training session early every morning of the week

Above: Ingrid Kristiansen trains on a running machine when snow prevents training outside

The two world-class Norwegian runners Ingrid Kristiansen and Grete Weitz have overcome the training difficulties of a cold climate

It is best to train on soft surfaces – in parks, and woods or on golf courses – they are less jarring on the legs and spine in repetition work

Local weather conditions may also influence your routine and in a very hot climate you may have to run earlier in the morning or later in the evening to avoid the most extreme heat. The opposite extreme – prolonged, intense cold weather also causes problems but there is always a way round difficulties if you are truly determined to succeed. The two great Norwegian runners Grete Weitz and Ingrid Kristiansen have shown how they can overcome difficulties when living in a cold climate. Grete has trained between 5am and 7am in Oslo as this was the only time when the snow-cleared roads in the centre of the city were free of traffic. Ingrid has run for long periods indoors on a running machine when the snow near where she lives has been too deep. One thing is certain – that few of the world's best runners have constantly enjoyed ideal training conditions.

2 Background support

A relaxed and supportive domestic background is most helpful to you, and understanding parents, husbands or wives are great assets to a runner. For example, Ian Stewart (European 5000m Champion and World Cross-Country Champion) used to tell me that he owed much of his success to his mother's ability to feed him properly and to see that he always had clean, well-washed running kit available.

The home background should be supportive and interested without being obsessive, but unfortunately some young athletes suffer from having over-ambitious and over-anxious parents. You should make sure that your parents appreciate the long-term aspect of your running development and do not expect overnight improvement or constant success. Having someone who understands what you are trying to achieve, be it parent, coach, boyfriend, girlfriend, husband or wife can play a major part in having a settled environment. If you are at school or at work, try to find a sympathetic teacher or boss who will appreciate and encourage your athletic aims.

3 Facilities

For a great deal of your running you will not need

much in the way of facilities – roads, woods or parkland are usually within easy reach, but it is worthwhile going out of your way to find a good-quality synthetic track on which to carry out your track sessions. Bad weather makes grass or cinder tracks unreliable and when you are planning sessions that have the specific aim of achieving fast times, then it is important to have the track on your side rather than against you. I have included some hill-training in my programmes and I would prefer that you used woods or parkland for these sessions rather than roads. Doing fast hill repetition on the road can be fierce on your feet and legs so it is well worth looking further afield to find a suitable surface or gradient. I tend to assume that hills are always close at hand but this assumption once let me down when I was organizing a training camp in Holland. I had allocated two hours for a hill training session but had to completely revise my ideas upon being told that the nearest hill slope was over 80 miles away and this was really only an apology for a hill as I knew it.

Track training can be beneficial provided that the runners are evenly matched with a similar fitness level, and that the session is not allowed to become too competitive

4 Coaching

Do you need a coach? As a coach, I have to resist the temptation to say yes unreservedly and instead say, "Yes – a *good* coach can help you a great deal". A thoughtful and imaginative coach will act as a tutor in your early days but will gradually introduce you and your ideas into the planning of training and racing. Eventually you and your coach will end up as partners. A coach needs to have a good technical and preferably practical knowledge of all aspects of running and also the ability to communicate this knowledge and experience to you. I like to think that athlete and coach very quickly become a team and do not go along with the master/servant relationship that prompts the coach to say, "You do the running – I'll do the thinking."

The good coach will be a shrewd assessor of ability and should be able to give you a good idea of your eventual potential. He/she should be able to motivate and inspire you at training sessions

and at races, and his/her presence should make you want to pull out all the stops. His objective should be to help you achieve your full potential and not to use you in order to further his own reputation. Above all, he needs to be absolutely honest with you, so that you can always rely on his predictions and decisions. You should respect his experience and judgement in the same way that he respects your ability and determination. As it is quite common for your coach to be with you most of your athletics career, I think it is important that you get on well together, both on and off the track. There is a lot of humour (much of it cruel sarcasm) that goes back and forth between coach and athlete so it is vital that you can enjoy a laugh together as well as be able to discuss the technicalities of training and racing.

Feedback sessions are important for the athlete and coach. Here, Steve Ovett and myself analyse a race's result, formations and tactics

I stressed that I thought a good coach would be a great asset and I must emphasise *"a good coach"* as I feel that no coach is better than a poor coach. The unimaginative or thoughtless coach can not only hinder your progress but by initiating bad faults and by non-constructive thinking can also affect the way that you would fare with a different coach. When you look for a coach remember that it is a unique one-to-one relationship. Go for someone who has the knowledge, is imaginative, honest, thinks positively and, in coach Franz Stampfl's words, can be a "guide, philosopher, friend". Do not just choose someone who has achieved results with someone else; check that the methods that he/she uses are based on sound principles. You need a coach who will be with you through thick and thin and not someone who will be enthusiastic only as long as good results are forthcoming. Communication between you should be a two-way process. Rather than you merely listening while your coach talks, play your part by passing on information about such things as: your feelings in races and training; information about your rivals' tactics and training; possible signs of illness or injury etc. Find out from your coach why you do particular sessions, what benefits are gained from certain types of training, how well you are progressing. Remember that just as a good coach can stimulate an athlete to good racing performances, so you can stimulate a coach to good coaching practice.

5 Training partners

As with a coach, you will find that good training companions are a great help whereas antagonistic running mates can be a nuisance and a hindrance. At times it is valuable to have someone with you on long runs or providing practical assistance during intensive repetition sessions, but you have to feel that your training partners are trying to help you and not attempting to beat you. While it is useful to have 'a bit of needle' during some of your training sessions, it can be destructive to have every session turn into a competition. Of course, as you improve, so you will find that the phrase the 'loneliness of the long-distance runner' becomes more pertinent. You will discover that no-one can stay with you on your long runs and that other athletes can do only a fraction of your

fast repetition sessions. This is the penalty you pay for getting better and something that you must accept. However, there are plenty of times when you train well within yourself and it is on these occasions when you will welcome company. I know that Steve Ovett benefited enormously from the companionship provided by Matt

Steve Ovett and myself contemplate the so-called 'Big Dipper' at Merthyr Mawr, Wales

Paterson on many of his training sessions, while both Kirsty Wade and Chris Benning pay full tribute to the help given by their husbands Tony and Martin as training partners.

CHAPTER TWO

TECHNIQUE

The full value of excellent fitness can only be realised when it is allied to a sound running technique, so it is no coincidence that all the current world record holders from 800m to marathon look good when they run. A good running technique should not only be mechanically efficient, but also economical. Some people will say that running is a natural activity so there is no need to worry about technique. I cannot agree with this. Running may be a natural activity, but running fast for prolonged periods is a different matter and I think it is reasonable to channel a runner's energy in the most efficient way possible. Endurance events are all about saving energy, not wasting it, so when you run, try to cut out all those actions such as head-wagging, arm-flapping etc. that waste energy and do not contribute anything towards running efficiently.

The way you run is dependent on several factors, some of which we can do very little about,

The training sequence below illustrates how runners can try to acquire a relaxed and mechanically efficient technique on the track. They all maintain good energy-saving, rear leg extension, and the athlete leading the pack uses an economical, relaxed arm movement

eg. the length of your limbs or the way that your bones are set in their sockets. But other factors such as muscle strength, limb flexibility and height/weight ratio also affect your running technique, and these can be influenced by training. A study of the accompanying running sequences will influence you more than anything I write, but it is important that I emphasise some of the points that contribute towards an efficient running technique.

All your drive should be in a forward direction
It is mechanically unsound to run with your knees turned either inwards or outwards. These results are usually caused by insufficient strength in the calves and/or thighs and I have illustrated some exercises for strengthening these below.

Hill running is my favourite way of improving leg-strength in runners and regular hill-repetitions are included in the schedules in Chapter 4. The runners I coach use two quite different types of hill-running and it is important that you adapt the correct running technique during these

Strength exercises

1 Exercises for improving strength and flexibility in calves and ankles: do 10 repetitions pushing as high as possible

2 Exercises for strengthening hamstrings. Hold the position for 10-15 seconds. As you get stronger lean slightly forward, keeping your back straight. Your calves must be held firmly

sessions, otherwise there will be little gain in strength. The first type of hill-running is carried out on a shallow slope (preferably short grass or a woodland trail) of approximately 10 to 20 degrees over a distance that can range from 300m to 500m. You try to run up using a normal technique (which actually means a higher knee-lift in order to negotiate the slope) and as soon as you reach the top of the hill you turn round and jog quickly down. It is vital to maintain a normal stride length and to check that your knees are pointing to the front. It is easier to take short quick strides and to turn the knees out but this will not help to give you stronger legs. You must remember that the objective of the exercise is to gain leg strength, not to get up the hill quickly. I recommend six to eight repetitions depending on the length of the slope, and that the whole session is completed without a break.

The other type of hill-running is carried out on a steep hill approximately 60-100m long and in this session you run with an exaggerated knee lift and arm drive. I suggest 8-10 repetitions with a slow walk-back downhill between each repetition. The photo on page 25 shows the recommended technique and on this occasion the runner has used a hill of soft sand which makes the activity harder. Once again there must be a conscious effort to keep your knees pointing to the front.

Hill running is my favourite way of helping runners to improve and develop their leg strength. Sandhills make the exercise more demanding

Good flexibility in the hips and ankles allows you to run more freely and with a greater range. Flexibility exercises are shown on page 28

Strong stomach and back muscles allow your torso to remain steady while your legs rotate underneath it and these areas must not be neglected. Exercises are given on page 30.

Your arms provide the balancing reaction to the movements of your legs and should swing backwards and forwards. However, your legs, because of the way they are set in your hip sockets, do swing in slightly to land in a straight line so your arms should also swing slightly across the body. Hands should be bunched, but not clenched tight, and I do not recommend flapping hands as these

1

2

4

3

General flexibility exercises

Jo White demonstrates five exercises that should be practised regularly. Hold positions for 15–20 seconds and repeat 3–4 times. These exercises have increased Jo's mobility tremendously. She is able to maintain a full range of movement within each position

1 Try to press your head against your knees while keeping your legs straight

2 Press gently against the right leg – switch to the left leg

3 With your back and rear leg in line, keep your heel on the ground. Hold the front leg high. Switch legs after 15–20 seconds

4 Keep the heel of the front leg on the ground and the rear leg straight. Switch legs after 15–20 seconds

5 Keep the raised leg straight and pull the toe down. Switch legs after 15–20 seconds

5

Strength and endurance circuit

Several of the athletes I coach like to include this circuit in their training programme, particularly during the pre-track competition phase. The three exercises are practised in the following order: press-ups, sit-ups and squat-thrusts. Start off by doing each exercise for 20 seconds, with a 20-second rest between each. Gradually build up your time to 60 seconds for each exercise, with a 60 second rest between each. When you can manage this, attempt 2 circuits and then 3 circuits etc. Take a two-minute rest between each circuit

***1 Press-ups:** use your arms to raise and lower your body, do not let your bottom sag*

***2 Sit-ups:** keep your feet on the ground and raise your trunk until your forehead is close to your knees*

***3 Squat-thrusts:** from a crouching position with palms on the floor, shoot your knees forward to reach your arms. Make sure when you thrust your legs back that they are fully extended*

lead to flapping arms. Your arms should swing loosely from the shoulders and be flexed at an angle of approximately 90 degrees. Over-flexed arms tend to lead to a cramped chest, whereas arms that are under-flexed make a long lever. These long levers require more energy to move them than the short levers of correctly flexed arms. Many runners are not particularly strong or flexible in biceps, chest, shoulders and back muscles so are unable to adopt the arm action I suggest. If this is the case, then I suggest using the three exercises shown on this page.

I often hear proud fathers shouting to young athletes at the end of races "use your arms". How can they when there just is not the muscle structure

1

2

3

Arms

Hold a light weight, such as a telephone directory, in each hand and keep your body steady while you do the following exercises:

1 Do 10 push-ups with each arm

2 Start with arms by your sides. Raise to the horizontal position: do 10 repetitions

3 Start with arms raised and held to the front, pull wide until level with your shoulders: do 10 repetitions

to drive their arms hard when they are tired? Much better that they should encourage their children to strengthen the relevant areas and then practise the required technique.

Your head should be carried naturally upright and you should look at the ground a few yards ahead of you. Throwing your head back or drooping your chin restricts your breathing and creates energy wasting tension in the neck and shoulder muscles. Do not waggle your head about as this interferes with your forward vision as well as wasting energy. Because you cannot hear the runners behind you on synthetic tracks there is occasionally a tendency to look over your shoulder. This is a dangerous thing to do. You may hit the kerb, run into the person ahead of you, or swerve into a runner alongside you. But if you are going to sneak a look behind, do make sure that it is only a quick one.

The pictures of Johann Boakes on page 22-23 show the technique I recommend for the main body of the race and you will see that there is an air of relaxation about the action. You can only 'run relaxed' if you are really fit. The fitness comes first, and then you practise running fast and relaxed. I have suggested some suitable relaxed running sessions in Chapter 6, 'Running Relaxed', and these not only save energy, but will also put you in the mental condition to respond to any sudden changes of pace during the race. Many runners fail to appreciate that they need to change their technique in order to surge or sprint at the finish. The normal 'swinging along' style needs to change quickly into a powerful driving style. The pictures of Zola Budd and Kirsty Wade opposite demonstrate two examples of good finishing technique.

The real test is whether you can hold on to a good finishing technique even when you are tired. You still need to maintain a long powerful stride and the driving arm action to match this stride. This is where the strength factor supplements the endurance factor. You need powerful thighs to lift your knees *high* and *straight ahead*: *high*, so that your driving leg has time to extend fully, and *straight ahead* so that none of your drive is lost in a sideways direction. You need to be strong in the calves so that you can drive powerfully and for a long time. Maintaining good form is par-

Zola Budd and Kirsty Wade – 1500m sprint finish

1 Zola's right foot, on the track, is in the middle of the supporting phase of the leg action. The outer ball of the foot struck the ground before the heel dropped lightly to the track to the 'flat-footed' position. This position is a solid base for the right leg's function of supporting the body's weight. The right calf muscle takes a rest for a fraction of a second. Zola's arms are relaxed and in line with her body but, viewed from the front, her elbows have swung outwards and could become entangled with Kirsty's arms

2 The body weight moves over and in front of the right foot and the right leg begins its driving phase. The left leg folds up to swing through with the left foot tucked up close to the buttock

3 The right leg driving phase is completed and Zola shows a fine range of movement. Extending the rear leg fully, using her foot as a lever, she continues the drive through the ball of the foot to the toes. Powerful thighs lift the leading leg high and allow the driving leg sufficient time to extend fully. Good hip mobility extends the leading leg well beyond the body. A powerful arm action should counteract this vicious drive. In ***4, 5 and 6*** *Kirsty and Zola allow their arms to straighten out of the flexed 90 degrees position. The long lever of a straight arm takes more energy than the short lever of a fixed arm*

4 Note the amount of ground covered as a result of powerful leg drive and hip mobility – Kirsty is about to land on the outside of the left foot. Tension in her neck and shoulders wastes energy. Feet and knees pointing to the front show good forward drive despite end-of-race fatigue. As the thighs become tired they turn out rather than drive up and forward impeding this forward directional drive

5, 6, 7, 8 and 9 *The cycle of the left leg drive*

1
2
3
4
5
6
7
8
9

ticularly vital at the end of the shorter races where several runners can finish within a second of each other. This is why I always make the runners whom I coach practise sprinting technique when they are still a little tired after an endurance session. Sprint coaches would not agree that this is the best time to practise this technique and I would go along with them if I was teaching technique to sprinters. However, there is a great deal of difference between sprinting from blocks when you are fresh and trying to sprint at the end of a gruelling 1500m or 10,000m. Sprint drills are mentioned regularly in the chapter on training schedules, and a typical session is featured opposite.

The important thing about technique is to develop an efficient action when you are young – it is difficult to alter a style that has been developed as a result of millions of repetitions of a particular action. If you cannot study a video or film of yourself, get someone to watch out for the points I have stressed. If you think that changes need to be made, do not procrastinate – start now.

Bounding and knee-high lifts

For specific instructions on the bounding sequence 1–6 (below) and the knee-lifts 1–6 (opposite) see sprint drills (below right)

Sprint drills

3 x 60m relaxed stride. Jog back between each stride.

3 x 60m starting slowly and gradually accelerating until you are sprinting over the last 10m. Walk back slowly between each effort.

3 x 30m high knee-lift (see sequence above). This exercise should be done slowly, emphasising the length of time that the leading leg is held high. As you become stronger gradually increase the distance covered to 60m. Jog back slowly between each exercise.

3 x 60m – bounding (see sequence on page opposite). A soft, even surface is needed as a flat-footed landing is recommended. Also try to maintain the long high-lift of the leading leg. Jog back between each effort.

3 x 30m very short, very quick strides. With this exercise you almost 'patter' on the spot, making very little forward movement. Walk back between each exercise.

3 x 60m split: 20m fast, 20m stride, 20m fast. Jog back between each run.

3 x 60m split: 20m stride, 20m fast, 20m stride. Jog back between runs.

3 x 60m sprint from standing start. Walk back slowly between each sprint.

CHAPTER THREE

TRAINING

In an earlier chapter, I outlined the two main energy processes that are utilized in endurance running (aerobic and lactic anaerobic) and it will be the development of these two processes that will take up most of your training time. Your major aims will be:

1 To increase your oxygen uptake so that you can run faster and further before going into oxygen debt. Your ability to recover quickly after going into oxygen debt will also be improved.

2 To increase your oxygen debt tolerance so that you can continue to run fast despite a build-up of lactic acid. Although training to improve these two factors will be your main aim, other aspects that have to be covered, according to the demands of a particular event, will be speed, mobility, strength and technique.

The balance between aerobic and lactic anaerobic training will depend on your racing event. The shorter and faster events will utilize the lactic anaerobic system much more than the longer, slower events, and getting this balance right at a particular time of the year is probably the most difficult part of planning your training. It may well be that a marathon runner could almost ignore lactic anaerobic training completely as this energy process plays only a tiny part in the event but at the other end of the endurance scale – the 800m – both types of training will be needed. A glance back to the graph on page 11 will remind you how fully both energy processes are used in the shorter endurance events. We can now consider how best to improve all the various factors.

Improving oxygen uptake (the endurance factor) One way of improving endurance will be to run over varying distances at speeds fast enough to have a training effect on the aerobic energy system, yet not so fast as to build up a lactic acid debt, ie. maintaining a balance between your oxygen uptake and the oxygen required to keep the activity aerobic. As you start to run, your heart begins to beat faster and harder. It needs to push out more blood with each beat and to push the blood around the body at a faster rate. You can use this heart rate as a measure of the intensity of your runs. Although you will vary the speed and distance of your runs, you will be running for most of the time in what is called a 'steady state'. This means your heart will have speeded up at the start of a run and then levelled off to stay fairly steady for the remainder of the run. Graph 2 (coloured line) illustrates this steady state effect.

These runs need to be of a certain intensity to bring about a training effect and it is this intensity that marks the difference between the fun-runner and the competitive athlete. Fun runners or joggers usually do not run sufficiently fast to bring about a training effect and are often quite happy to be sociable and stay in groups while they are running. You will need to base the pace of your runs on your own fitness at any particular time. If this fitness coincides with that of other runners, then it is quite useful to train with this group, but if the other runners are too fast or too slow, then staying with them will not produce the correct training effect. If we accept that the coloured line on Graph 2 was the effect produced by Mr A, a 5000m runner capable of 15min 30sec, can you imagine what would happen if the author (now a typical middle-aged, overweight ex-runner) tried to stay with Mr A on a run? My pulse rate would rise quickly, fail to level off and continue to rise until the point at which I would be heavily into oxygen debt. I would then have to slow down until my pulse rate stabilized and then I could continue at my own pace. The black line on Graph 2 would reflect my run and this certainly

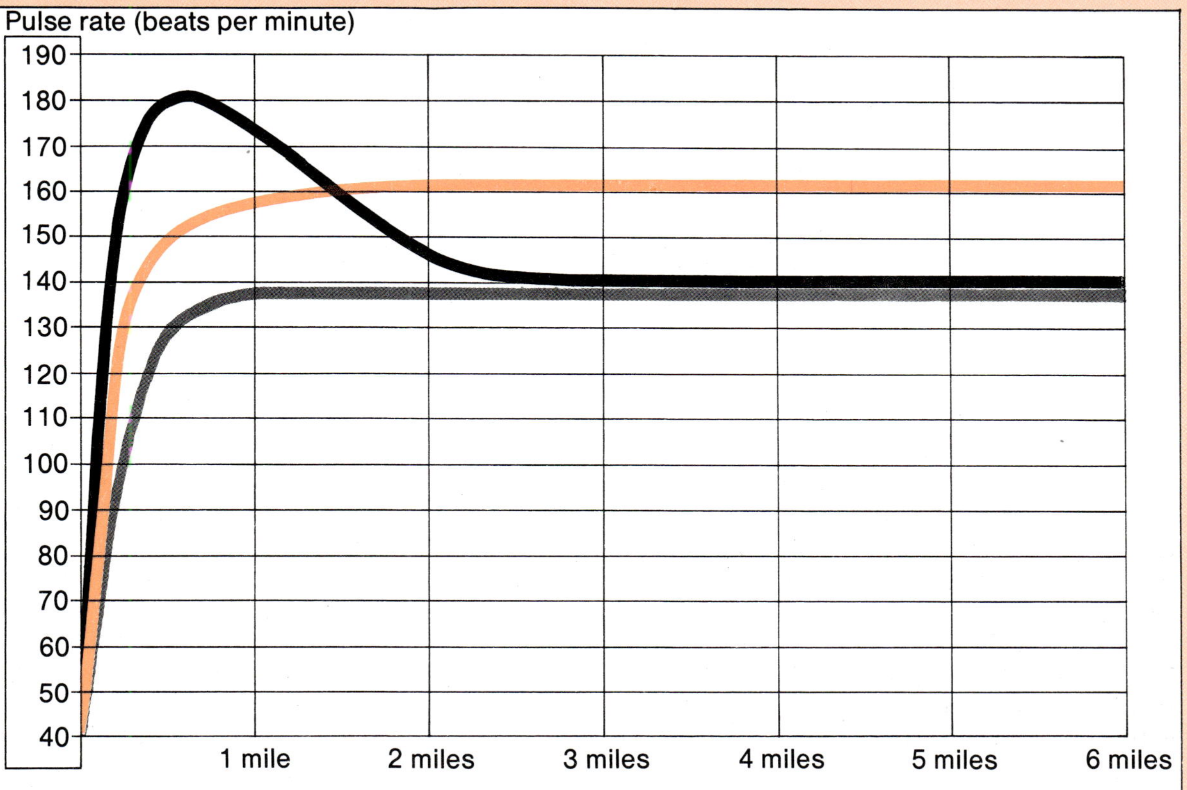

Graph 2: pulse rates during a six-mile steady-state run for three different runners

could not be described as a steady state run. Alternatively, let us imagine that Mr B (a 13min 30sec 5000m runner) decides to run alongside Mr A on this 5-mile run. Because of his extra fitness, his heart rate would not rise very high in order to run at this particular pace and would probably be reflected by the grey line on Graph 2. This run would not benefit Mr B much as the effort involved would not be sufficient to bring about any real training effect.

You have to find your own individual training threshold and ensure that a fair proportion of your steady state runs are at or above this threshold. A simple but fairly accurate way to determine your training threshold is to use the following formula:

1 Take note of your maximum pulse rate expressed as so many beats per minute. A really fast 200m or 300m would produce the right effect.

2 Take your resting pulse rate, again expressed in beats per minute. A good occasion to determine this would be when you are lying in bed first thing in the morning.

3 Deduct the resting rate figure from the maximum rate figure, and then calculate what is two-thirds of this remaining figure.

4 Add this calculation to your resting rate figure and you then have your training threshold.

As an example, we can examine the way this formula worked out for Josephine White, one of the runners I coach. She is an international class runner with personal bests of 2min 2sec for 800m and 4min 10sec for 1500m, so as expected has a low resting pulse rate of 48 beats per minute. Her training threshold formula would be:

Maximum rate – 190 beats per minute
Resting rate – 48 beats per minute
Deduct the resting from the maximum rate – 142

Two-thirds of 142 is 95 so if we add this to her resting rate of 48 we have a training threshold for Josephine of 143 beats per minute. She uses this formula as a guide to the pace of her steady state runs as follows: she tries to use a pace for her 5-mile runs that will give her a steady state pulse rate of 155/160 beats per minute. For her 10-mile runs she aims for a pace that produces a steady heart rate of 145/150 beats per minute.

If you refer back to the coloured line on Graph 2, you will appreciate that such an evenly shaped steady state curve is not really accurate, as to produce this effect would mean that the course should be perfectly flat, the pace absolutely level and not a breath of wind present. In fact, there are heart rate fluctuations taking place as a result of such factors as changes of pace, increases in the strength of the wind and the effects of running up and down hills. These factors bring about minor fluctuations without detracting from the main aim of the exercise, ie. to run at an effective aerobic level for a long period without incurring any significant oxygen debt. Accepting this point enables you to develop the aerobic energy system without adhering strictly to steady state runs. A typical example of another form of aerobic training would be as follows:

Six fairly steady runs over 1000m with only a short recovery jog of 30 seconds between each run. A reflection on the heart rates produced during this training session is shown in Graph 3. All sorts of distances can be used for this type of training session but the principle remains the same, ie. the faster repetitions should not be so fast as to produce any significant oxygen debt while the recovery jogs are too short to allow the heart rate to fall any appreciable amount.

Distances to use for aerobic training differ from event to event and according to the time of the year. My recommendation, along with suggested training loads, is given in Chapter 4 which covers all aspects of the training plan.

Improving oxygen debt tolerance (the speed/endurance factor)

The general objective of this type of training is to run hard enough to produce an oxygen debt, have a partial recovery and then repeat the exercise a number of times. There are several ways of achieving this effect but the basic principle remains the same – fast efforts interspersed with recovery periods. Once again you can use your heart rate to monitor the effects of your training, and Graph 4 gives you an idea of the pulse rates likely to be achieved during a typical speed/endurance session. By comparing the pulse rate curve shown in Graph 4 with those displayed in Graph 2 you can readily appreciate the totally different training effect being achieved by the two different types of training.

The methods you use for improving your oxygen debt tolerance will depend on such factors as: time available, facilities available and personal preference for a particular training surface. However, whatever method you use must be influenced by the following principles:

1 The amount of lactic acid built up in the fast runs depends on the speed and duration of the efforts. This factor, in turn, influences the amount of recovery needed to re-convert the lactic acid to glycogen.

2 As you are trying to persuade your body to adapt to conditions that apply in a race, the intensity, duration and number of fast efforts attempted should relate to your racing event. They should also relate to your level of fitness at a particular time in the year's training plan. For example, I would not recommend that an 800m runner in his/her competition period contemplate a session consisting of a large number of longish repetitions run slowly. Yet this sort of session could be relevant at another time of year.

3 Your body takes rather a long time to recover completely from a very intense speed/endurance training session so I would recommend a gap of at least three days between this type of session and an important race. For example, if you are racing on Saturday, your last intensive speed/endurance session should be no later than the previous Tuesday.

Having established the general principles, we can now examine some of the methods used to improve lactic acid tolerance.

Fartlek (a Swedish word meaning speed-play)

With this type of training you run for a period of time, usually over undulating ground such as parks, woods or golf-courses, alternating varying stretches of fast running with sections of jogging. Although the objective is to run fast when you feel like it, Fartlek is not an easy form of speed/endurance training. Although you have no set patterns of fast sections or recovery sections, only you and your conscience can make Fartlek sufficiently intensive to be effective. The accompanying sketch will give you an idea of a typical Fartlek session and you can see that it will

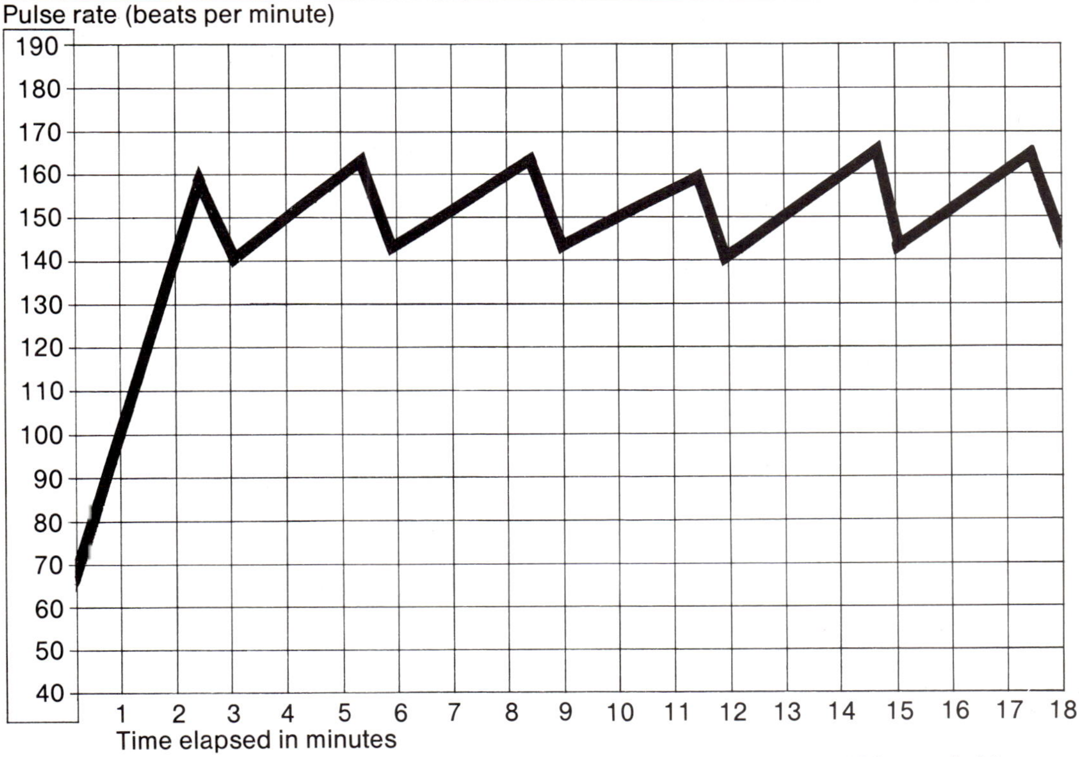

Graph 3: pulse rates during a high-quality aerobic session – 6 x 100m with 30 sec recovery between each

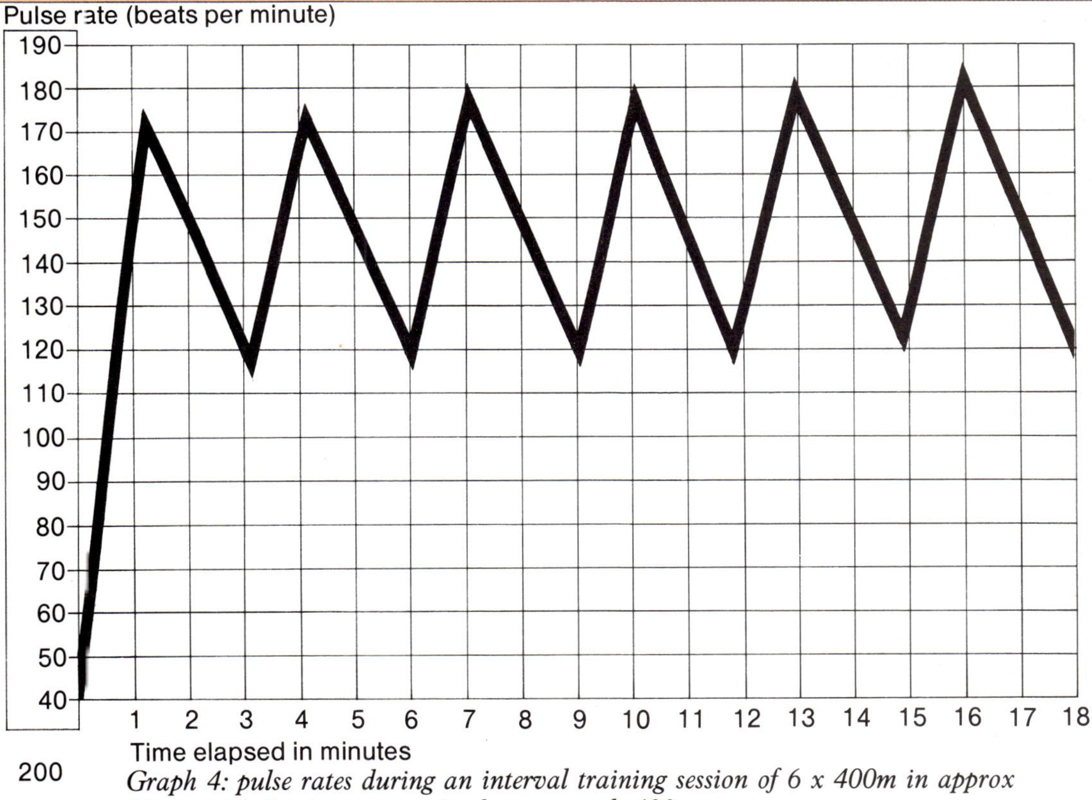

Graph 4: pulse rates during an interval training session of 6 x 400m in approx 60 sec with 2 min recovery jog between each 400m

produce varying severities of oxygen debt.

It is important to use the 'make it progressive' principle with Fartlek so if you start running this type of session at the beginning of March then you should be gradually intensifying or lengthening the fast sections as the weeks go by. Although Fartlek is often used to make a break from the more formal methods of improving speed/endurance, it must not be regarded as easy or recuperative. This is why it is a form of training

probably best suited to the more experienced runner who has the discipline to make each session effective.

Interval training
This term is now used to cover a whole multitude of variations on the theme of alternating short fast runs with fairly short recovery periods. Originally used in the 1920s, the concept was formalized by the German partnership of coach Gerschler and physiologist Reindell in the 1930s and 1940s, and it is now used in one form or another by most middle-distance runners all over the world. The original Gerschler/Reindell concept was to select a particular distance for each session (usually 200m, 300m or 400m) and to repeat this distance a set number of times at a predetermined pace. The recovery time allowed between fast sequences was also predetermined and the Germans used the athlete's heart rate as the parameter for deciding the pace to be used and the recovery to be allowed. Athletes were expected to achieve a heart rate of 180 beats per minute at the finish of each fast sequence and 120 beats per minute at the end of each recovery period. These two figures have become the accepted criteria used by coaches when monitoring the intensity of most interval training sessions, but some coaches (myself included) will on occasions ask runners to go beyond the 180 top figure and also start up again before the 120 low figure has been reached.

A typical session as used by a good class 1500m runner would be written down as:
8 x 400m (58sec) with a 200m jog (90sec) as a recovery.

Graph 4 shows the heart rates likely to be recorded in this particular session. As the runner improves in both oxygen intake and lactic acid tolerance, he can probably achieve the 400m in 58sec with a lower pulse rate. The heart rate would also probably be capable of reaching 120 beats per minute recovery target in less time than that originally planned. When the runner is able to reach his original targets for this particular session on three occasions, I would apply the basic principle of progression and want him to make the session harder. He could do this by either:

1 Increasing the distance used for the fast sequences.

2 Increasing the speed of the fast sequences.

3 Reducing the recovery time between fast sequences.

4 Increasing the number of fast sequences.

However, the concept of progression is not so simple as it seems. Take the runner featured in Graph 4. It is reasonable to expect that after successfully tackling this session on three occasions he would achieve his target of 58sec for each 400m with a pulse rate of only 174 beats per minute. This should also lead to the target recovery rate of 120 beats per minute being achieved after 75sec. If we decide to develop this session by making him run each 400m in 57sec, thus pushing the pulse rate up to 180 beats per minute, then he may need the full 90sec to reach the target recovery rate. Alternatively, if we decide to improve the session by reducing the recovery time to 75sec, so that his pulse rate is then 120 beats per minute just before the start of each fast 400m, then it is likely that he will record 180 beats per minute when he does the 400's in 58sec.

Increasing the distance run to 500m would probably achieve the effect of producing a heart rate of 180 beats per minute, in which case we would probably let the recovery period stand at 90sec. Increasing the number of repetitions from 8 to 12, while maintaining the same speed and recovery time, will not achieve the intended 180/120 heart rates but would enable the runner to operate at a lower level for a longer time. This effect may have more value for runners in the 5000m and 10,000m events.

In general, I like to think of 800m/1500m runners intensifying this form of interval training by increasing either the speed or by stepping up the distance of the fast stretches. With 5000m/10,000m runners, I would be inclined to progress these sessions by reducing the recovery time while maintaining pace and/or by increasing the number of repetitions.

Intensifying or modifying interval running sessions is not only influenced by your progress, but also by the particular stage you have reached in your yearly training plan. For example, in the Spring phase you could progress by cutting down recovery times or by increasing the number of repetitions, whereas in the Competition phase you would be more likely to opt for increased

The top-class international 10,000m runner Julian Goater has benefited greatly by switching from long-mileage, high-volume running to high-quality interval running

speed or for lengthening the distance of the fast sequences. What you must always consider is the objective of the session. For example, if you are concentrating on the speed of the repetitions, do not try also to go for short recoveries. Conversely, if you wish to keep the recoveries short, do not keep trying to achieve very fast repetitions. If the aim of the session is to build up a large number of repetitions, then do not expect to record really fast times or to achieve very short recoveries.

The speeds at which you aim and the recoveries allowed are influenced mainly by the pulse rate parameters mentioned earlier, whereas the distances chosen and quantities planned are related to your main racing distance. You cannot hold pace for very long once your pulse rate starts going above 180 beats per minute so this will condition the length and speed of your repetitions. In addition, you ought to feel that the technique you use in training is similar to the one used in racing. When we use the track for interval running, we tend to take advantage of the track markings to determine the distances used, eg. 200m, 300m and 400m, but there is no special significance about these distances. It is the effect you achieve that is important. I, along with other coaches, use woods, fields or parks for interval running, and the circuits are invariably of odd distances. For instance, in the woods near my home the athletes I coach use circuits that measure 325m, 590m and 780m. What matters is that circuits produce the required physiological effect while providing a change to the track.

Although the original concept of interval running was to select a particular distance and recovery time and stick to these throughout the training session, there are now several ways of achieving the required effect and here are some typical examples:

Variation on distances

A typical session used by Julian Goater (13min 17sec for 5000m), one of the athletes I coach, is 3 x 800m (at his 1500m pace), 4 x 400m (at his 800m pace), 5 x 200m (at his 400m pace) with the appropriate recovery time after each fast sequence.

Sets

Occasionally, if you have a largish number of repetitions to complete in a session, it can help you to retain concentration and to maintain good quality by breaking the session up into a series of sets. Thus for a 5000m runner, instead of attempting 15 x 400m with 200m jog in between, he could change to three sets of 5 x 400m with 200m jog between each 400m, and 400m jog between sets.

High intensity intervals
Some years ago, two of the athletes I coach, Tony Summers and Steve Ovett, told me that they felt that the normal type of interval running took too long to achieve the required effect. In a session of 12 x 300m with 200m jog as recovery, they only really experienced difficulty in the last two or three repetitions. This was despite meeting the pulse rate targets of 180/120 beats per minute. This was due partly to their bodies' adaptation to several years of high-quality training, and partly to them being accustomed to experiencing very high pulse rates in many of their races. So we adopted the method of running sets of small numbers of very fast repetitions with only a short recovery between the fast runs, but a significantly longer recovery between the sets. A typical session for Tony (fourth in the 1976 Olympic 10,000m) would be 6 sets of 4 x 400m in 58/60sec with 30sec between each 400m and 4/5 minutes' rest between sets. The pulse rates achieved in this type of session are reflected in Graph 5 and give quite a different picture to those shown in Graph 4.

As my description suggests, this is an extremely intense type of training which is probably best suited to the more experienced runner. You need courage to run the first sequence in each set really fast for you know that with such a short recovery, the second run in the set is going to hurt a lot. You destroy the objective of the session if you protect yourself by saving yourself on the first run of each set. After the first fast run you need great concentration to hold yourself together during the short recovery, and then you must dig deep into your determination reserves to make the second run fast. You then need great discipline to inflict this form of torture on yourself more times during the session. I certainly would not use this type of training more than once a week and not before an important race. However, I am convinced that these sessions can be valuable by the fact that runners tell me that although they do not look forward to this type of training, they feel very satisfied when the session has been completed.

Relaxed intervals
In the earlier chapter on technique, I stressed the importance of learning to be relaxed when running fast. This technique can be practised in a particular form of interval running that I like athletes to use during the competition session. When you have used a certain interval session several times and have progressed it by the usual methods, you can develop it in another way: ie. by maintaining pace while trying to run as relaxed as possible. For example, if in Spring, you started running a session of 8 x 300m in 48sec with a 2-minute recovery jog between each 300m, then it is likely that within two months you will have progressed to 8 x 300m in 42sec. You could then use this as a 'relaxed interval' session in between races by trying to maintain the 42sec pace with a smooth relaxed action. You do not press hard to try to run the 300's in 40 or 41sec; you try to maintain 42sec with less effort than before. Concentrate on keeping your pulse rate low while still running fast. You will know if you are progressing, not because you are recording faster times, but because you are clocking up 42sec with less effort. If you wanted to run faster, you could, but you are saving this extra pace for races. A reminder – running relaxed means running fast without tension. It does not mean running slowly nor does it mean running sloppily. Study the running sequences on pages 24-25 and try to achieve this type of relaxed technique.

Repetition running
Although the basic principle involved is similar to that of interval training, we have come to associate Repetition Running with the use of longer distances and longer recoveries. This is logical, as holding the heart rate at a fairly high level for several minutes necessitates allowing extra time for it to return to an acceptable recovery level. I find this type of training most valuable at the beginning of the competition phase when I recommend a small number of high-quality repetitions with a lengthy recovery time between each run. This recovery could be a mixture of walking and jogging. A typical session for a 10,000m runner could be 3 x 2000m (at 5000m race pace) with 4/5min recovery between each repetition. High quality is an important factor

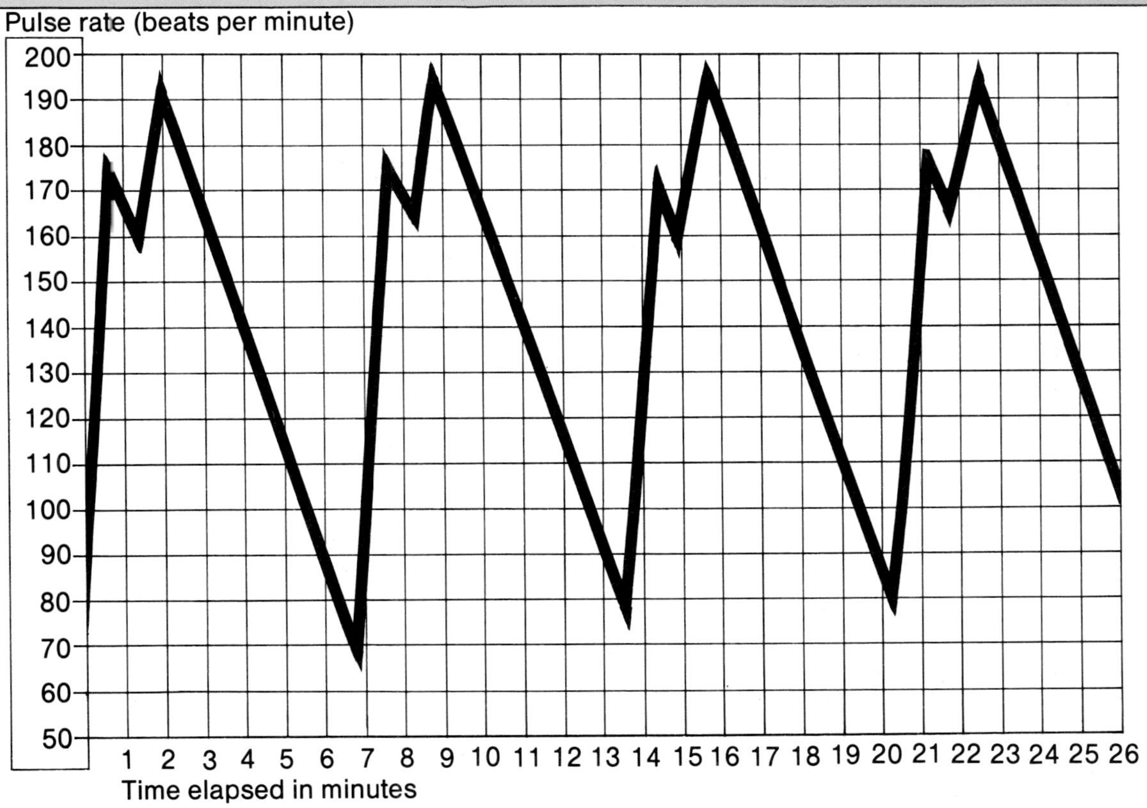

Graph 5: pulse rates during a high-intensity training session of 4 sets of 2 x 300m (approx 40 sec) with 30 sec rest between each 300m and 5 min rest between each set

with repetition running so ensure that the pace chosen for a particular distance is as fast or faster than that section of your main racing distance. For instance, Billy Dee (a 7min 49sec 3000m runner) would run 4 x 800m in 2min with a 4/5min recovery period. Once again I stress that if you are aiming for quality, you cannot expect to have short recoveries or a large number of repetitions. Much better for a woman 1500m runner aiming for sub-4min 10sec performance to achieve a session of 3 x 800m in 2min 12sec with 6/7min recovery than to run 3 x 800m in 2min 18sec with 3/4min recovery.

I think that this is the right place in the book to stress the importance of self-analysis. Ask yourself before training sessions, "What's the object of this exercise?" Then when the session has been completed, ask another question: "Did I achieve the objective?" Similar questions ought to be asked before and after different phases of the training year.

The quantities and distances to use for interval training and repetition running are related to your racing event and the time of the year but the examples I give in the chapter on training schedules will provide a good guide.

Race practice

With this form of training, you are attempting to reproduce the circumstances and feelings that occur during races. Typical occurrences are:

1 A much faster start than expected.

2 A sudden surge or surges during the main body of the race.

3 A gradual increase in race-pace. All these occurrences can be simulated in training.

I like athletes to start including this type of session just before the beginning of the competition phase and to continue with the session throughout the racing season. I have described some race-practice sessions that my athletes use and the accompanying sketches will give you an idea of what is required.

Split intervals In this session the first section of each repetition is run at below race-pace, then the second section at above race-pace. You can increase the pace of the second part of each run either by: building up the pace gradually; or surging hard and trying to hold the new pace. The diagrams show some suggested split-interval sessions for various events.

800m runner (personal best 2min) 3 x 400m split. 200m steady (32/33sec): 200m fast (27/28sec): 4/5min recovery between each 400m.

1500m runner (personal best 4min) 4 x 600m split. 300m steady (51/52sec): 300m fast (45/46sec): 4/5min recovery between each 600m.

5000m runner (personal best 14min) 6 x 800m split. 500m steady (85/86secs): 300m fast (49/50sec): 5/6min recovery between each 800m.

10,000m runner (personal best 31min) 5 x 1200m split. 800m steady (2min 33sec): 400m fast (70/71sec): 5/6min recovery between each 1200m.

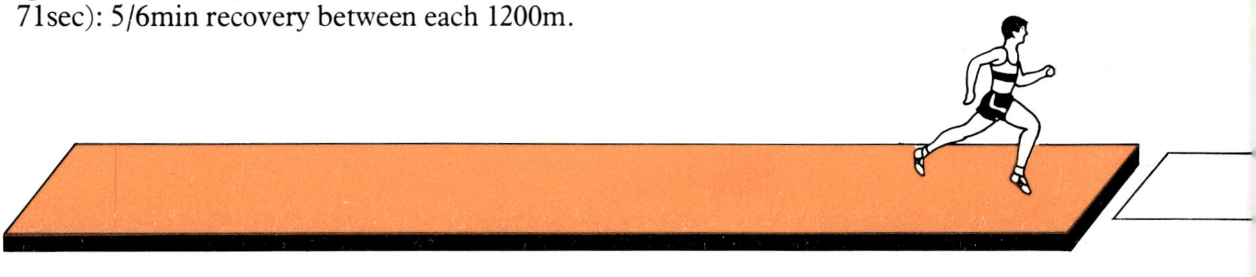

You aim to run relaxed over the first section of each run and then change your action to gain speed over the second stage. You will need to concentrate on holding back on the first part of each run, for if you go too fast you will not be able to accelerate on the second stage and the objective of the session will be lost. Long recoveries are needed to ensure that your heart rate has sufficient time to come down to 120 beats per minute.

Tired surges The first part of the repetition is run at a fast pace. This is followed by a short jog which only gives you a partial recovery. Then comes an attempt to surge into a fast finish even though you are feeling tired. Typical sessions are as follows:

800m runner
400m fast (slightly faster than race-pace): 100m jog: 100m sprint. I suggest four repetitions with a full recovery (6/8min) between each run.

1500m runner
800m fast: 100m jog: 200m fast. Three or four repetitions are suggested with a full recovery being allowed.

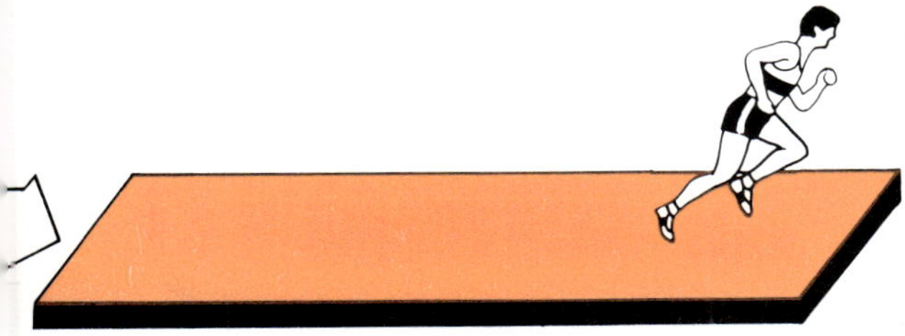

5000m/10,000m runner
1200m fast: 200m jog: 400m fast. I suggest two or three repetitions with again a full recovery of 6/8 min being allowed.

Pace injectors With this type of repetition you 'cruise' the first section at race-pace, then surge hard during the middle section, and ease back to race-pace for the final section. The two sections illustrated in the sketches are:

800m/1500m runner
4 x 600m divided into three sections: 200m at race-pace: the next 200m at 2/3sec faster than race-pace: then 200m again at race-pace. Allow time for full recovery between each repetition.

Steve Ovett

5000m/10,000m runner
4 x 1200m divided up as follows: 400m at race-pace: 400m at 3/4sec faster: then 400m at race-pace. I suggest a recovery lasting 5/6min between each run, but this time must be governed by your pulse rate.

This particular session was used most effectively by Steve Ovett in 1986 when he was making the transition from 1500m to 5000m as his main

Top-class runners who follow my schedule are are always poised to handle a change of pace within a race. Correct training prepares them to cover any eventuality that may arise within the course of a 5000m or 10,000m race

racing distance. A typical session for him was 4 x 1200m with the 400m splits being 63sec: 58sec: 63sec. His recovery time would be 4/4½ minutes.

I feel that this session has special relevance to 5000m/10,000m runners. It assimilates a common race occurrence where you accumulate a small oxygen debt after a fast surge and then have to recover quickly when the pace settles down again.

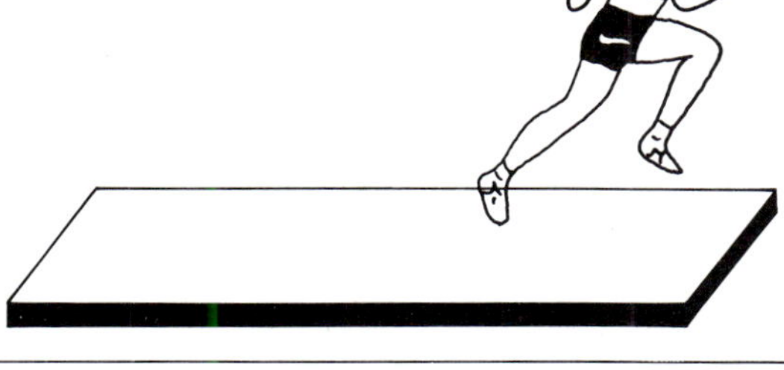

Pace increasers The objective here is to become familiar with the feelings you experience in a race which is run with a gradual increasing pace and is most relevant to 5000m/10,000m runners. Two typical sessions are:-

1500m runner aiming for a 4 min performance: 6 x 600m aiming for three consecutive 200m to be run in 34sec, 32sec and 30sec. Recovery complete when heart rate is down to 120 beats per minute.

5000m runner aiming for a 14 min performance: 4 x 1200m aiming for three 400m laps to be 70sec, 67sec and 64sec respectively. Allow plenty of time for a full recovery.

This chapter has given you details of various activities that will form the bulk of your training; the following chapter lays out how these activities fit into an overall yearly training plan.

CHAPTER FOUR

THE TRAINING PLAN

By now you should have a pretty good idea of the various ingredients that combine to make 'the training cake'. What is now needed is a recipe that will use these ingredients in the right quantities at the right time. The right time is in races. An effective plan is one that gears your training towards producing good results in races that count. It is no good running like the wind in May if you have run out of steam by the time that your target races come around in July, and it is pointless being in world record form in October if the racing season finished in September.

I believe that a runner should have a general plan that will lay down the emphasis that is to be placed on a certain aspect of training at a particular time. This chapter outlines this 'macro-cycle', while later on in Chapter 6, you will find some schedules which form small parts of this plan – 'micro-cycles'.

I realise that I am attempting the impossible by suggesting a plan that will suit athletes from many different environments and with varying levels of ability, but I feel sure that once you appreciate the reasoning behind the plan then you will be able to prepare a plan that will suit your own individual circumstances and aspirations.

The plan that follows has in mind an athlete living in the Northern Hemisphere who wishes to race well at cross-country during February/March and then again on the track from mid-June to September. Further on in this Chapter, I have given alternative plans for three other racing programmes:

1 The runner who wants to race indoors instead of cross-country.

2 The athlete involved in the American college competition scene.

3 The athlete competing in the Australia/New Zealand programme.

The overall plan for Northern Hemisphere

Endurance phase
(include cross-country competition

Winter
October to mid-March
24 weeks

Pre-track competition phase

Spring
Mid-March to early June
13 weeks

Track competition phase

Summer
Early June to Sept
13 weeks

The endurance phase

The first part of the plan involves building up a very solid endurance background for all the various distances. This concept has been the one used by 95 per cent of all successful British runners in recent years.

Experience has taught me to emphasise the endurance factor first before working on the speed/endurance factor, but there is nothing new about this belief. This approach was the one used by Walter George (World Mile Record Holder) as long ago as 1896; by Sydney Wooderson (World 880 yards and Mile Record Holder) in the 1930s; and was stressed again by the highly successful New Zealand coach Arthur Lydiard in the 1960s and 1970s.

It takes a long time to develop endurance which is why I stress such a long and gradual build-up in the first stage of the plan. It is no good being very fast in May if you are short of endurance – you will not have time to develop the staying factor before the track season is upon you. The first priority in any endurance event is the ability to last the distance at a good pace. What is the point of being able to run a 400m in 48sec if when the bell sounds in a 10,000m race you are a lap behind?

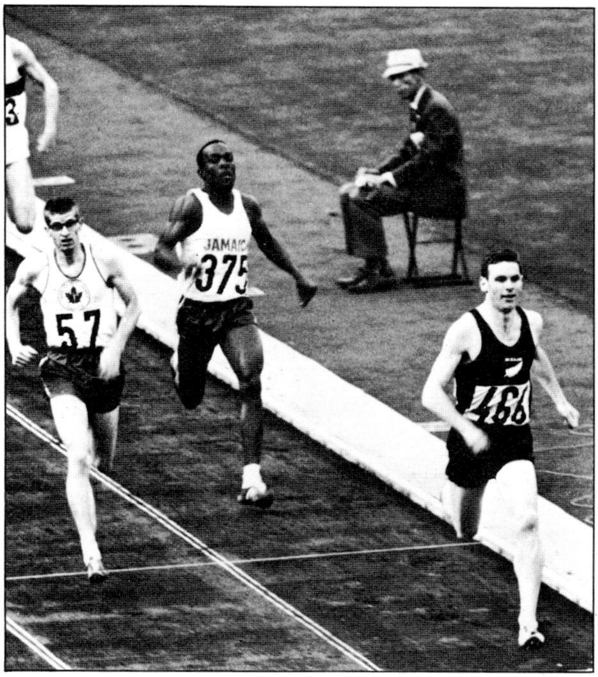

Sydney Wooderson (top) and Peter Snell (above), who was coached by Arthur Lydiard, both successfully used the endurance factor in their races on the athletics track

The long and gradual build-up enables you to hold on to the endurance factor even when you have had to reduce this part of your training in order to develop other aspects.

The objective of the endurance phase is to improve your oxygen uptake, and this factor alone will mean that you are better equipped to tackle the more intensive speed/endurance work that follows in the next stage of the plan. You will see from the chart that as the endurance phase progresses, a change takes place in the quality of the steady-state runs that provide the bulk of your training. At the start of the period most of the runs are at the lower end of the aerobic scale (ie. just above the training threshold), but as time goes by you will gradually include more runs at a higher aerobic level (probably 12-15 beats per minute above the threshold rate).

There is a small anaerobic content in the training carried out during the first phase as it is important to remind your body of the other energy process. You will also experience some oxygen debt at various times during hard road or cross-country races. I also include a small amount of pure speed work in the endurance phase. I think it is useful to keep the fast-twitch muscle fitness ticking over and to retain the sensations of the sprinting technique. I also suggest including some technique drills and leg strengthening exercises on the occasions when you do speed work. The balance of training during the endurance phase is shown in the table.

Endurance phase

OCT	NOV	DEC	JAN		FEB	MAR
4 weeks	**4 weeks**	**2wks 1wk 2wks**	**4 weeks**	**1wk**	**4 weeks**	**2 weeks**
AEROBIC (light load Low Level 100%	AEROBIC (increased load) Low level 95% Med/high level 5%	AEROBIC (increased load) Low level 80% Med/high level 20% NB. 1 week of reduced load low level aerobic in middle of this periods.	AEROBIC (increased load) Low level 75% Med/high level 25%	Reduced load – low/med level	AEROBIC (reduced load) Low/med level 70% High level 30%	AEROBIC (reduced load) Low/med level 70% high level 30%
		ANAEROBIC Speed/techn.	ANAEROBIC Speed/techn.		ANAEROBIC Speed/techn.	ANAEROBIC Speed/techn.

During the endurance phase you are progressing by judiciously varying:

1 The distance and number of your runs.

2 The pace of your runs.

You must be careful not to attempt both at the same time. When you look ahead to a week's training you can plan your progression by thinking "on Sunday and Wednesday I'll increase the distance run; on Monday and Thursday I'll try to increase the pace." Do not forget that during each week there should be at least one recuperation day, and even though you may like to run on this day you should ensure that it is an easy relaxed run. Although distance covered is only one criteria to use when developing the endurance phase, it is useful to have a plan showing how you intend to build up the distance covered in this period. Here are some examples of quantity plans:

800m/1500m runner (training once a day

2 weeks	–	20 miles each week
2 weeks	–	30 miles each week
4 weeks	–	36 miles each week
2 weeks	–	2 miles each week
1 week	–	25 miles each week
2 weeks	–	42 miles each week
4 weeks	–	48 miles each week
1 week	–	25 miles each week
4 weeks	–	48 miles each week
2 weeks	–	42 miles each week

800m/1500m runner (training twice on same days)

2 weeks	–	20 miles each week
2 weeks	–	30 miles each week
4 weeks	–	50 miles each week
2 weeks	–	60 miles each week
1 week	–	30 miles each week
2 weeks	–	60 miles each week
4 weeks	–	70 miles each week
1 week	–	30 miles each week
4 weeks	–	80 miles each week
2 weeks	–	60 miles each week

5000m/10,000m runner (training once a day)

2 weeks	–	25 miles each week
2 weeks	–	35 miles each week
4 weeks	–	40 miles each week
2 weeks	–	45 miles each week
1 week	–	25 miles each week
2 weeks	–	55 miles each week
4 weeks	–	65 miles each week
1 week	–	25 miles each week
4 weeks	–	60 miles each week
2 weeks	–	50 miles each week

5000m/10,000m runner (training twice a day)

2 weeks	–	25 miles each week
2 weeks	–	40 miles each week
4 weeks	–	60 miles each week
2 weeks	–	70 miles each week
1 week	–	30 miles each week
2 weeks	–	75 miles each week
4 weeks	–	90 miles each week
1 week	–	35 miles each week
4 weeks	–	75 miles each week
2 weeks	–	65 miles each week

In each plan I have included recuperation weeks at strategic points and would use another similar week at the end of the phase. It is much better for you to plan to take these easy weeks rather than to be forced into them because you feel a bit jaded and need a break. You will be fortunate if you manage to complete this endurance phase without having to take some time off owing to illness or injury. If you do have to miss your training for a few days, do not try to make up for lost time by drastically increasing your mileage. Some athletes become unreasonably worried if they have to miss a few days' training and seem to think that months of regular running can be wiped out by a day or two of enforced rest. If this happens then all the principles of exercise physiology need re-writing. From my observations, I see very little loss of fitness for anything less than 10 days' loss of training. There is a gradual decline in your fitness level for longer periods of time off and when this happens you will need to have another look at your original plan and see how best to rearrange your schedule in order to include any specific factors that may have been neglected.

There are other athletes who become so paranoid about daily training that they are afraid to take advantage of easy days or weeks. Again, this is a failure to understand one of the principles of exercise physiology, ie. recuperation can be just as vital as hard training.

You will notice that I have suggested a reduction in the training load during February and March. This is to enable you to approach the peak of the cross-country season in the right physical and mental condition. No doubt, you will want to take part in cross-country or road races earlier on in this endurance phase, but these should be tackled without any significant reduction in your training load. However, these races will give you a clue as to the effectiveness of your training programme so allow for a slight easing down before any important competition.

During the endurance phase you will need to adopt the correct mental approach, such as: "It's not the success of a particular day or a particular week that's important; it's the completion of the period as a whole that counts". I like athletes to be able to look back at their training diaries in March and say: "Just look at that little lot – no great sessions or great weeks, but a whole period of solid training." You treat each session as a brick in the solid wall of endurance that you are building.

The pre-track competition phase

This is the most difficult part of the year to plan as your training becomes more varied and intense. It is a period that will call for a great deal of mental effort. In the previous phase, which was mainly endurance-based, you gradually became used to the feelings of fatigue peculiar to aerobic running. Now you will be experiencing also some new aches and pains as you start to incorporate other activities. It is vital in this phase to know yourself well and to be clever enough to modify your training should you become over-fatigued. A different mental approach is needed, particularly towards the end of the period when you are at the stage where intense physical and mental concentration is required to get the most out of each effort in each session. The balance of training has to be right in this phase or there will be few opportunities to make drastic changes to your programme once the competition phase begins.

This is also the period when you are at the stage where intense physical and mental concentration is required to get the most out of each effort in each session. The balance of training has to be right in this phase or there will be few opportunities to make drastic changes to your programme once the competition phase begins. This is also the period when you could benefit most from the assistance of a good coach or a perceptive friend. Some runners are self-motivating, but many others need some external motivation in order to get the best out of themselves in quality sessions. Because of the intensity of the training, the pre-competition phase tends to be the one that leads to the most injuries so before this period starts, make sure that you have located a good physiotherapist and a doctor experienced in sports injuries. My suggested balance of training for the period is as follows:

800m runner

March	April		May	June
(3wks)	(3wks)	(1wk)	(3wks)	(3wks)
Endurance 60% Intervals or fartlek 30% Speedwork 5% Strength & mobility 5%	Endurance 50% Intervals or fartlek 40% Speedwork 5% Strength & mobility 5%	Recuperation week of easy runs easy intervals, relaxed speed-work	Endurance 40% Repetitions 25% Fartlek 25% Speedwork 5% Strength & mobility 5%	Endurance 35% Repetitions 25% Fartlek 25% Speedwork 10% Strength & mobility 5%

1500m runner

March	April		May	June
(3wks)	(3wks)	(1wk)	(3wks)	(3wks)
Endurance 70% Intervals & fartlek 20% Speedwork 5% Strength & mobility 5%	Endurance 65% Intervals & fartlek 25% Speedwork 5% Strength & mobility 5%	Recuperation week of easy runs easy intervals, relaxed speed-work	Endurance 60% Intervals & fartlek 15% Repetitions 15% Speedwork 5% Strength & mobility 5%	Endurance 54% Intervals & fartlek 12% Repetitions 12% Speedwork 5% Strength & mobility 5% Race practice 12%

5000m/10,000m runner

March	April		May	June
(3wks)	(3wks)	(1wk)	(3wks)	(3wks)
Endurance 80% Intervals & fartlek 16% Speedwork 2% Strength & mobility 2%	Endurance 75% Intervals & fartlek 21% Speedwork 2% Strength & mobility 2%	Recuperation week of easy runs easy intervals, relaxed speed-work	Endurance 70% Intervals & fartlek 13% Repetitions 13% Speedwork 2% Strength & mobility 2%	Endurance 66% Intervals & fartlek 10% Repetitions 10% Race practice 10% Speedwork 2% Strength & mobility 2%

You will see that, once again, I have specifically included a recuperation week in the middle of the phase. In addition, there will be easy sessions included in the weekly schedules that are detailed in a later chapter. This easy week is the time when you assess how well you have performed/ progressed and decide whether there is any need to alter the balance of training for the following six weeks. Towards the end of the period I recommend that you include two or three low-key races. I would advise you to take great care in your choice of training shoes as you make the

transition from the endurance phase to the pre-competition phase. During the endurance phase you will have spent most of your time wearing fairly heavy shoes, with thick spongy soles that give your legs a lot of protection. As you start to include the faster speed-endurance sessions, take care that you do not wear lightweight, thin-soled spikes on all of these sessions. Most of the lightweight shoes offer very little protection for your legs and introducing them gradually can reduce the risk of incurring two common injuries – shin-soreness and conclivities of the achilles tendon.

At the end of the pre-competition period you will have completed the bulk of your intensive training and can look forward to adopting a different approach towards your running in the coming competition phase.

Track competition phase

Although the main training aim in this period is to maintain fitness between races, there is still a certain amount of improvement that can be made by the use of specific sessions. Your training should be sufficiently comprehensive to maintain all the various aspects of fitness, yet not so severe that it takes away the freshness that is needed to produce good race results. Bear in mind that there is a certain amount of training effect to be gained from racing – there is no surer way to get the exact aerobic/anaerobic balance.

Kirsty Wade, Yvonne Murray, Christine Benning and Liz Lynch are four British women who have made it to the top of international women's athletics

In fact, I know top-class runners who deliberately arrive at this stage of the year about 90 per cent fit and count upon a few fast races to top up the remaining 10 per cent. Race-practice sessions and relaxed interval sessions will help you maintain sharpness and concentration without the mental stress of competition. When you do these particular sessions remind yourself of the objectives involved. It is not good sense to keep on trying to produce 'personal best' training times two or three times a week and also produce your best racing results, yet some athletes seem hell-bent on this self-destructive approach. There is an old gardening adage that "you don't dig up the roots to see if the plant is still alive." Yet some athletes keep on testing themselves to maximum in training despite the assurance of good racing results. Easing the training load before a competition in order to be fresh, both mentally and physically, shows positive thinking; in fact, many runners tell me that they have in-built protective systems that automatically switch on prior to an important race. It is also sensible to follow up a particularly hard race with an adequate recovery period.

Thinking along these lines means that if you are racing every week, then you need to allow a minimum of three days to cover the pre-race relaxation, the race itself, and the post-race recuperation. This leaves only four days each week for training of which probably only two days are of any level of intensity. So there is a distinct possibility that if you were to maintain a race a week for too long, you could start to lose some of your fitness. The general endurance aspect will probably be the area that suffers most, so in the depths of winter when you might be tempted to say "Why am I spending so much time on endurance?", remember that it has to last you throughout the competition period. You cannot suddenly include a couple of weeks of long endurance runs in a period that is aimed specifically at quality.

I would prefer to counter the risk of losing endurance by making athletes divide the competition phase into periods of frequent racing, alternating with battery recharging periods. I suggest 20/21 day racing periods followed by 9/10 day 'topping-up' periods.

A training plan for this period becomes very much an individual affair depending on such factors as:

1 The quantity and quality of the races you can obtain.

2 The travelling involved in getting to and from races.

3 How much time you personally need for pre-race relaxation and post-race recuperation.

4 How well you personally manage to maintain fitness with a reduced training load.

Rather than produce a balance of training chart as I did for the other two phases, I think it is preferable to refer you to the typical race build-up plans that are described in the training schedules in Chapter 6. Success during the competition phase depends as much on your mental state as on your physical condition, and belief in the soundness of your training will go a long way towards building up your self-confidence. Your training diary should provide evidence of how thorough and conscientious your training has been. Along with the confidence that should spring from the evidence of your diary, should come the urge to race. I like athletes to *want* to race and to *want* to show people just how good they are. Preparing for a race is like preparing for an exam. You know the questions that are going to be asked – make sure that you have prepared well and know the answers. When you feel that you have the answers, then you will have no fear of examinations or races. I know some runners who are almost afraid of racing. The fear of losing or running badly seems to lie so heavily on them that they would gladly pull out of a race if offered a good excuse. I find this very sad and feel sure that a lack of confidence in the training programme must have some bearing on this fear of failure.

Some of you may wish to race indoors rather than compete in cross-country races, in which case I recommend the year plan below:

This plan is most suited to the shorter endurance events and has produced good results for Kirsty Wade, Britain's most successful 800m/1500m runner both indoors and outdoors.

It is essential that you follow the indoor competition phase with a topping-up period of endurance running. This training should be biased towards fairly fast steady-state runs and high-quality aerobic repetitions. There is a natural reluctance for a runner who has been training and racing at a high intensity level for some weeks to return to less intensive endurance work. However, many top runners have told me that if they neglect this period they feel that they are running out of stamina before the end of the outdoor track season.

Overall plan to cover indoor and outdoor track competitions

Endurance phase	Pre-indoor competition phase	Indoor competition period	Endurance phase	Pre-outdoor competition phase	Outdoor competition period
Oct to mid-Dec 10 weeks	Mid-Dec to end Jan 7 weeks	End Jan to mid-Mar 7 weeks	Mid-Mar to mid-Apr 5 weeks	Mid-Apr to early June 8 weeks	Early June to Sept 13 weeks

Here Kirsty Wade challenges for the lead in the 1987 World Indoor Championships women's 1500m race in Indianapolis, USA

American college competition

The North American competition schedule with its series of fairly short racing periods sets the college runner quite a difficult problem when it comes to preparing a training plan. In particular, this is the case for the many American runners who now travel to take part in the European track season as soon as the TAC and NCAAA championships are over. It is difficult to fit in heavily loaded endurance phases that last long enough to have a really sustained effect, as, quite naturally, most colleges expect scholarship athletes to produce good competition results for most of the year.

The plan I suggest recognises these problems by balancing the aerobic/anaerobic ratio more evenly throughout the year and by training in two- week cycles during the two track competition periods. During these two-week cycles there will be more endurance training than at a similar stage in a European runner's plan. The plan has worked well for several runners whom I advise who are based in the USA, and enables them to compete in both the European and American track programmes. Suggested schedules for the different phases within the plan are included in Chapter 6 covering schedules for individual events.

Australian and New Zealand competition

The cross-country and track competition seasons are very long in these countries but the plans I have prepared are aimed at athletes peaking in September for cross-country, and March for track.

The overall plan
Endurance phase (includes cross-country competition) Mid-April to end of September 24 weeks
Pre-track competition phase October to end of December 13 weeks
Track competition phase January to end of March 13 weeks

The suggested balances of training during the endurance and pre-track competition phases are given earlier in the chapter and Southern Hemisphere runners will just need to make amendments to the months quoted in order to use these Training Balance Charts. These runners will then be able to use the schedules for the individual events that are quoted in Chapter 6. The 14-day cycle of training to use in the competition period is also featured in Chapter 6.

Overall training plan for North American runners

Sept	Oct	Nov	Dec	Jan	Feb	Mar	Apr	May	Jun

Cross-country competition						Indoor competition		Outdoor competition
6 weeks Gradual build-up, mainly endurance. 90% aerobic 5% anaerobic 5% SP ST	Easy week	**3 weeks** Continue build-up or endurance. 80% aerobic 15% anaerobic 5%SP ST	**4 weeks** Maintain quantity, more quality. 75% aerobic 20% anaerobic	Easy week	**5 weeks** Pre-indoor comp period. Training balance according to event.	**8 weeks** 4 x 2-week training cycles according to event	Easy week	**10 weeks** 5 x 2-week training cycles – balance according to event

SP: Speedwork
ST: Strengthening work

CHAPTER FIVE

TACTICS

I asked a well-known runner what he thought was meant by the phrase 'running tactically'. His answer was that 'a tactical run was one that was won in a slow time even though the competitors could all run much faster'. I suppose that this is a commonly held view. My view is that the tactics you use are those that enable you to take full advantage of your strengths to run up to your level of fitness at a particular time. You have to know yourself well to adopt this approach, and it also helps to have some knowledge of your opponents' strengths and weaknesses. Of course, in many instances you will know very little about your opponents, or you may have *some* knowledge of your rivals but may not be aware of their level of fitness at a particular time. So self-knowledge is the most important factor and you should ask yourself the following question: "Am I best-suited to being a front-runner or a follower?" This is a psychological question as well as a physical one. Although many runners are forced into being front-runners because they lack a finishing burst, there are others who are quite well equipped to handle a fast finish yet still feel happier when they are leading a race. However, it is usually a shortage of basic speed that makes you a front-runner, and if this applies to you, then you should consider some ways of running that will help you to combat the efforts of the strong finishers.

The front runner

First, being a front runner means being prepared to run up to your maximum, so if your fitness is at all suspect you should not try to dominate a race from the front. If you are happy with your fitness, then you should weigh up just when you are going to take the lead and set the pace. If you decide to 'go from the gun' this establishes your belief in yourself and from then on your job is either to shake off the rest of the field or to make the pace so fast that even if there are runners near to you in the closing stages of the race, their speed will have been nullified by the intensity of the pace you have set. Leading from the start enables you to dictate the pace of the race and ensures that the pace is sufficiently fast to damage your rivals, yet not so fast that you damage yourself.

You can run to a time schedule, in which case I would suggest an even-paced schedule based on a time a little faster than your personal best. Alternatively, you can start a little slowly in order to allow your body time to adjust to the increased work-load, and then gradually pile on the pace as the race develops. This is a hard way to run, but it is even tougher for the followers who keep wondering, "just when is this pace going to slow down?" Another way is to go off a little faster than even-pace schedule in an attempt to break clear of the field, but if you try this you must be sure that your oxygen uptake is so high that you can get rid of the small amount of lactic acid that will have accumulated and then settle down to runnning at the top end of your aerobic scale for the rest of the race. You should also not run too fast and incur such an oxygen debt that you have to slow down and thus allow the other runners to catch up and probably go past.

David Bedford, the former World Record Holder for 5000m and 10,000m was a great exponent of the very fast start (he usually opened up with two laps of 60 secs) and once he had broken away he possessed the will-power and fitness to keep on running at a fast enough pace to prevent his rivals from closing the gap. However, on those occasions when his opening gambit failed to open up an immediate gap, he seemed to lack the concentration to continue running hard in

order to gradually wear down his rivals. If you decide to run from the front at a steady pace right from the gun, you must not be discouraged if your rivals stay with you for a long time – you have to credit them with a fair fitness level. In which case, it may only be in the final stages of the race that the effects of your wearing-down tactics start to show dividends, eg. the last 150m

The fast-starter David Bedford powers his way forward to break the world 10,000m record at Crystal Palace stadium in London

of an 800m race, or the last 1000m of a 10,000m race. During the major part of the race you must not waiver in your intent, and if you do not win, then at least you know you were beaten by someone who just happened to be fractionally better than you on the day. You will not have to go away thinking, "I've been beaten by someone who was nowhere near as fit as me but just happened to have a bit more basic speed".

However, I must stress that it is no good leading a race at a gentle pace solely because you like being at the front. If you set a gentle pace and have no finish, you will be taken apart in the closing stages. Remember the basic rules of the front-runner: try to break away *or* try to take the sting out of the fast finishers. You do not have to lead from the gun to apply these two rules. If you run in a race that is being led by someone else at

Said Aouita of Morocco hits the front half-way through a race. Here he wins the 1984 Olympics 5000m gold medal

Lasse Viren (on the left) of Finland was another 5000m runner who never led from the start of a race but was always a 'stayer'

an adequate pace, you can afford to wait until you feel that the time is right before going to the front and applying a lot of pressure. I can think of several 5000m runners who did not want particularly to lead, yet who did not possess a really fast finish. These runners usually waited until after the 3000m mark had been passed before making their presence felt. Murray Halberg, Lasse Viren and Said Aouita are typical examples from the 5000m ranks.

Another way to make life uncomfortable for the fast finishers if you are a front-runner, is to inject a series of fast bursts during the race. These bursts must be long enough, hard enough and frequent enough to make the followers wonder about the wisdom of staying with you, and also to damage the speed of the fast finishers. It is not enough to throw in a couple of fast 200's and think that will be sufficient – it won't. If you are going to make it uncomfortable for your rivals, then it has to be tough for yourself, too. Using this tactic calls for the ability to withstand repeated pain and probably means that you need to practise plenty of high-intensity interval running.

If you are a front runner you are at a real disadvantage on a windy day and your efforts seem even more difficult when you realise that you are pushing hard into a strong wind while other runners are using you as a wind-break. If the wind is really strong, then I suggest that you wait until the last half of the race before going to the front, *or* you can try the ploy of surging hard with the wind behind you and then relaxing into the wind.

The fast finisher

If you do not like leading and have sufficient evidence to show that you are a fast finisher, then ask yourself the question: "Which type of finish suits me best – the short burst, or the longer steady drive for home?" Of course, you are ideally equipped if you can handle both types of finish, but most athletes prefer one or the other. If you are best suited to apply the long steady finish then you must ensure that, once you have started your finish, there is no let-up, and that your technique will not deteriorate right at the very end of the race. Holding technique during a prolonged finish demands that you maintain a long fast stride, so make sure that you have not

The short finish calls for a sudden change of pace – a few short powerful strides – fast enough to take you to the front and, because the finish is only a short distance away, just enough to prevent your rivals catching you. This type of finish also calls for great leg strength and mobility and the ability to alter technique quickly. You can practise by running relaxed and then suddenly changing technique to produce a few fast powerful strides.

If you are able to switch on both types of finish then the pace of the race or the finishing characteristics of your rivals will determine which option you choose. As a general rule, if the pace of a race has been very fast then keep the finish as short as possible. However, you may decide to break this rule if you feel that a longer finish would hurt your opponents more than it would hurt you. To know when to start your finish, you must have knowledge of your opposition, possess the physical characteristics to finish fast, and be sufficiently mentally aware to seize an opportunity and strike at the right time. Thus your mind must be active throughout a race – covering moves made by the opposition and making your move decisively and at the right time. This is where mental fatigue is linked closely to physical fatigue – you cannot expect to be on the look-out for openings if you are absolutely flat out just holding on to the pace. So possessing a fast finish does not give you a licence to neglect your endurance – the more endurance you have, the easier it will be to apply your finish.

During the writing of this book, I was talking to a woman international 800m runner who was considering moving up to 1500m because she did not possess a strong enough finish. She told me that she did a great deal of sprinting over 80-100m so she could not understand why she lacked a fast finish. I was fairly well-acquainted with her training and told her that I thought her problem was not due to lack of speed, but to low endurance and leg strength. I felt that she was arriving at the 600m mark with insufficient reserves to enable her to turn on her speed, and that her legs were not strong enough to maintain a long, fast stride when she was tiring. Before finishing the book, I spoke to her again and she told me that her finishing speed had improved enormously since she started incorporating into her training some high knee lifts for leg strength, and fast repetitions over 1000m for endurance.

To make the best use of a strong finish means positioning yourself cleverly so that when you do want to 'turn on the tap' there are no bodies in the way. During the main part of the race you want to position yourself where you can run smoothly

Below: Peter Elliott (9) front-runner, wins the 800m final in the AAA Championships 1987
Opposite: a glorious moment as Steve Ovett (279) wins the 800m final at the 1980 Olympics

and not be restricted, ie. you do not want to have to shorten your stride to avoid running into the back of someone; you do not want someone continually catching your heels from the rear; nor do you want to be constantly tangling arms with people on either side of you. So you should take up a position on the shoulder of one of the leading runners where you can sense any change of pace and respond without restriction. If after the start you find that this position is not vacant (the runners may already be two abreast) then just tuck in at the rear of the leading group. Keep your wits about you and when an opportunity to move up occurs without expending too much energy, then do so. Having established a good position, protect it by moving up or out if you feel threatened – this is particularly important as you start to near the crux of the race. This is the time when everyone is starting to get ready for their final surge, and it is vital that you are able to move freely at this stage. Two particular crux points are: just coming up to the bell in a 1500m or 1 mile race, and entering the back straight in an 800m race. You can usually sense when sparks

This photographic sequence shows a battle on the track between Steve Ovett, John Walker, Philip Deleze and Thomas Wessinghage. Steve Ovett is in an ideal position to strike and take the lead as he can respond rapidly to the leader making a break or match any challenge from an athlete on

his shoulder. He is covering Wessinghage on the inside and John Walker on the outside, while Deleze is boxed in and thus does not represent a threat. Note that he is also perfectly positioned to make a burst giving himself a free run on the outside of the leader. If this is the case, Wessinghage will not be able to respond sufficiently fast on the inside. Look at frames 8-13 where Ovett senses that John Walker is surging forward and responds immediately.

are about to fly, so be prepared and in position to move quickly. Another golden rule of tactical running is: "Once you have started your finishing burst, carry it through to the finish." It is tempting when you have made a break to ease up and look behind you. Forget it. If an opponent comes up on you fast, it is difficult to change technique and speed up again.

Despite all your good intentions, there are going to be occasions when you find yourself boxed-in on the curb with runners all around you. If this happens at an early stage in the race, do not panic. Wait until the slightest gap appears and then step out smartly and hold on to your new position. Some athletes prefer to slow down until they have been passed by all the field, come out at the back and then work their way up to the front again. However, there is a risk that while you are slowing down to carry out this manoeuvre the leaders may speed up and you will be left behind. But this may be the only choice left to you, in which case drop back smartly and then

Another shot of the Moscow Olympics 800m final with Seb Coe trying unsuccessfully to ease his way through on the outside and Steve Ovett poised

ease your way quickly on the outside up to the front again. If you are boxed in coming up to the crux point in a race, then quick drastic measures are necessary, for if you miss 'the break' there is little likelihood of you being able to get back in touch again. A typical example of this was Seb Coe's plight in the 1980 Olympic 800m final. There are ways of breaking out of the box but you have to take care that you do not break the rules. You can try to hustle the runners in front by running really close to them, and this may persuade them to run faster and create a gap for you to slip through. If you see the slightest gap on the inside in front of you then you can pretend that you are going to try to slip through it. This usually causes the runner in front to close in on the kerb which may then leave a slight gap on the right for you to wriggle through. If there is a runner to your right who is stopping you from breaking out, then you may have to indicate to this runner quite firmly that you are coming out anyway. You can edge over to the right and as you elbows start to get entangled the runner usually says, "I'm not going to take risks – if you want to come out that badly I'll give way." I've actually known runners stick out their right arms as though they were motor-car indicators and shout, "I'm coming out now". If things are getting desperate and there are two people side-by-side in front of you, you cannot afford to wait until the slightest gap occurs. You can either push both arms together in front of you and say "coming through" or twist your shoulders sideways and try to slip through. Most runners tend to think, "This runner's dangerous; better get out of his/her way". These are desperate measures to adopt but sometimes you either try them out or accept that you are not going to win.

Developing concentration

Earlier in this chapter, I sugested that whether you are a front-runner or a follower depends as much on your mental approach to racing as on your physical attributes. So, you will need to have great mental concentration whichever of the two options you choose to adopt. The front runner needs to be thinking positively along the lines of, "This is what I'm best equipped to do. I get my satisfaction from breaking away from my opponents – drawing the sting out of the fast finishers." It is no good being resentful if no-one else will take the lead, or taking the attitude that the fast finishers are parasites. They have a job to do – sticking close to you. I can remember one British Championships 1500m race which was won by a woman I coach and she achieved this by following closely on the heels of a woman quite renowned for her endurance and then sprinting past her in the last 50 metres. The runner who had led the race walked past me afterwards and, with great bitterness, spat out, "That girl's a creep – she runs like a ...... leech." I replied, "I'm glad you said that – she ran the race perfectly."

Just as much concentration is needed by the fast finishers for you have to stay in contact whatever the pace telling yourself, "No matter how tired I am, I'm still going to raise a sprint at the finish." At times you will need the nerve and patience to wait until the right opportunity occurs to begin your sprint, and it is easy to panic and either wait too long or start sprinting too soon. However, being a fast finisher does not give you the right to neglect the endurance side of your event. On the contrary, you need just as much endurance as the front-runner if you are going to stay close no matter what the pace.

Know your opposition

Although a few athletes may say that they do not know, or do not wish to know, anything about the opposition, I really feel that this is a subterfuge. You do not race in a vacuum and you cannot ignore the strengths and weaknesses of your opponents when planning your races. Weighing up the likely tactics of your rivals is a form of mental rehearsal and helps you to react quickly as tactical moves take place during a race. However, you must not become obsessed by your opponents – you can bear them in mind – and should always try to run to *your* strengths. As you approach a race you must remember that you cannot affect the fitness of your opponents and you cannot make them run slower. Your fate is in your own hands. However, by running intelligently you can get the best out of yourself and maybe influence the way in which your rivals perform. The clues you are looking for when assessing your opponents are:

1 Which runners prefer to lead and which prefer to follow.

2 Which runners prefer a short fierce finish and which are best in a long finish.

3 Which runners like to lead and are unhappy if they lose the lead.

4 Which runners are unhappy in a crowded situation and are afraid of any form of physical contact.

5 Which runners can be relied on to react violently if their running space is threatened.

6 Which runners will give up when they are passed and which ones will fight all the way to the finish.

7 Which runners will try to crowd you or constantly snap at your heels.

There are other factors to bear in mind but these seven points will give you an idea of how to assess your rivals. I think the best way for me to close this chapter on tactics is to look back at three classic races at different distances and see how tactics affected the results.

BRASIL
093
Games of the XXIIIrd Olympiad
385
359
USA
909

Above and right: the 1980 Olympic 1500m final in Moscow. Coe surged past Straub 100m from the finishing line to win the gold medal, but Ovett could only manage the bronze behind Straub who took the silver

Opposite: the Brazilian Joachim Cruz wins the 800m final at the 1984 Los Angeles Olympics. When Konchella began to flag, Cruz surged past him to win convincingly

800m: the 1984 Olympic Final

This was an example of one man, Joachim Cruz, dominating an event both mentally and physically. Prior to the Olympics, Cruz had given warning that he did not believe in slow 800m races and sure enough in the first round he signalled his intention of running all his races extremely fast. As soon as his intentions were known (he talked freely to the press) his rivals began to hope that they could steer clear of him until the final. Poor Steve Ovett drew Cruz in all three preliminary rounds. As each day went by and Cruz reeled off one fast run after another you could hear his rivals say, "Surely all these hard races must have an effect on him." Eventually you sensed that his opposition were not thinking along the lines of how well they might run in the final but were counting on Cruz running poorly. In fact, he did not take the lead immediately in the final; Konchella from Kenya had set off at a very fast pace, but as soon as he sensed that Konchella was flagging, the Brazilian surged to the front and opened up quite a commanding lead by the time he reched the tape. His four consecutive fast races were certainly the most powerful display of 800m running that I had ever seen, and just as significant was the way in which his aggressive running undermined the confidence of the other runners.

1500m: the 1980 Olympic Final

After the preliminary rounds it was obvious that this was going to be a three-man final – Steve Ovett, who had already won the 800m comfortably by seizing an opportunity when it occurred; Seb Coe, who had run aimlessly in the 800m and had never positioned himself well enough to win; and Jurgen Straub from East Germany, who had showed his physical capabilities when running a very fast semi-final against Ovett. The first 700m were covered at a very leisurely pace, and then Straub took off to run what was probably the fastest 800m in a championship race. Coe immediately tagged on to Straub while Ovett took up position on Coe's shoulder. The order stayed the same until with just over 100m to go, Ovett moved up to overtake Coe, who sensed the move and accelerated at the same time to go past Straub. Ovett now found himself with less than 100m to go trying to pass Straub who had responded to Coe's surge and also trying to close the 2-3 metres gap that Coe had opened up on Straub. The pace of the last 800m made the task too much for him and he had to settle for third place. Coe was in the ideal spot – when he made the final effort he had only one man to overtake. When Ovett started his effort, he was trying to get past two men who were already running very fast. In this instance, the position of Coe and Ovett as they approached the crux of the race proved absolutely vital. Praise must also go to Straub for his intelligent, brave running which brought him the silver rather than the bronze medal.

5000m: the 1976 Olympic Final

Brendan Foster, who had broken the Olympic record in what seemed an unnecessarily fast heat, led for the first five laps at quite a brisk pace, then Lasse Viren went to the front and slowed the pace down for the next 1000m. By doing this he spoiled Foster's plan for a sustained fast pace and also prepared the way for his own finishing tactic. Foster went into the lead again at 3000m and tried to break the field with a surge. Unfortunately, the fast heat had taken its toll – he could only sustain the surge for 200m and this tactic failed to get rid of his rivals. Lasse Viren took the lead again with about 1000m to go and started a remarkable sustained finishing pace. He ran a lap in 62.5 seconds and then took another in 60 seconds; yet still with just over 200m to go there were five men right on his heels. All of these men possessed faster 800m and 1500m times than Viren yet failed to make an impression on him during the last 200m which he covered in just outside 27 seconds and came home a winner by three metres. The stayer had beaten the fast finishers by clear thinking, positive action and an unshakable belief in his ability to wear out the 'sprinters'.

These are just a few examples of the way that some athletes have used different tactics. I hope that you will now appreciate the need to 'run cleverly' as well as to be in the peak of physical condition.

Brendan Foster(364) of Britain leads Lasse Viren of Finland in the 1976 Olympic 5000m final, but in spite of his inferior finishing speed Viren went on to take the gold by virtue of being a stayer and wearing down the traditional fast-finishers like Foster

364

CHAPTER SIX

TRAINING SCHEDULES

Most coaches are expected to write out training schedules in the way that a doctor writes out a drug prescription for an ailing person. Often at an athletics meeting, I am approached by a proud father who says, "Did you see my daughter win the 800m this afternoon? Well, she is only sixteen and can do 2min 15sec. Can you spare a few moments to write her out a training schedule?" I wish it was that easy. There are so many things you need to know about a runner before you commit yourself to writing a training programme and it is certainly not a five-minute exercise. It is not possible for me to have a long discussion with each of the many runners who will (I hope) buy this book and yet I feel that you should have some examples of the way that my ideas on training come together in training schedules. So I have prepared programmes for each of the standard track events and have envisaged two quite different athletes (both in standard and time available) for each event. Examine them carefully to see if they would suit you and your circumstances, and if you wish to make changes, do ensure that the basic principles of exercise physiology form the basis of your changes.

Will these schedules make you a champion? No self-respecting coach would guarantee you that, but I am confident that if you follow these guidelines, you will be a well-conditioned runner. After that it is up to you – I cannot run races for you. My job as a coach is to get each athlete into the right physical and mental condition to race well. It is then the athlete's job to make sure that racing performances reflect his/her fitness level. I must stress again the need for patience. It is unreasonable to write to me saying, "I followed your schedule for three months and didn't improve." I do not write the rules governing adaptation to training and although in most instances the athletes I coach have shown improvement within a year, it could take much longer with some runners.

800 metres

Schedules for a runner with a personal best of 2min 4sec, able to train once each day, aims to race cross-country at club level occasionally during the winter and to race on the track once every two weeks in the summer.

Endurance phase
October to mid-March – 24 weeks

October First two weeks – 5 miles easy steady-state run on Monday, Wednesday, Friday and Sunday.
October Second two weeks – 5 miles easy steady-state run on Monday, Tuesday, Thursday, Friday; 10 miles easy steady-state run on Sunday.

November Each week – 5 miles medium steady-state run on Monday and Wednesday; 6 miles easy steady-state run on Tuesday and Thursday; 4 miles fast steady-state run on Saturday; 10 miles easy steady-state run on Sunday.

December First two weeks and last two weeks.
Monday – 7 miles medium steady-state run.
Tuesday – 5 miles fast steady-state run.
Wednesday – 8 miles easy steady-state run.
Thursday – 7 miles medium steady-state run.
Friday – rest day.
Saturday – 6 x 1000m circuit (aim for 150/160 pulse-rate), 1 min jog recovery between each; 20 min rest; 15 min mobility exercises; 30 min sprint drills.
Sunday – 10 miles easy steady-state run.
December Middle week (recuperation week) – 5 miles easy steady-state run on Monday, Tuesday, Thursday, Friday and Sunday.

January First four weeks.
Monday – 8 miles medium steady-state run.
Tuesday – 6 miles run split-up – 4 miles fast, 1 mile easy, 1 mile fast.
Wednesday – 10 miles easy steady-state run.
Thursday – 8 miles medium steady-state run.
Friday – rest day.
Saturday – 6 x 1000m circuit, 30 sec jog recovery between each; 20 min rest; 15 min mobility exercises; 30 min sprint drills.
Sunday – 10 miles easy steady-state run.
January Last week – 5 miles easy steady-state run on Monday, Tuesday, Thursday, Friday and Sunday.

February 4 weeks.
Monday – 8 miles medium steady-state run.
Tuesday – 4 x 1500m circuit (aim for 150/160 pulse rate), 2min jog recovery between each; follow this with 3 miles easy run.
Wednesday – 10 miles easy steady-state run.
Thursday – 8 miles run split up: 6 miles steady; 1 mile easy; 1 mile fast.
Friday – rest day.
Saturday – 6 x 1000m circuit – 30 sec recovery between each; 20 min rest; 15 min mobility exercises; 30 min sprint drills. On alternative weeks substitute a cross-country race or 5k to 10k road-race for the above session.
Sunday – 10 miles easy steady-state run.

March First two weeks.
Monday – 6 miles medium steady-state run.
Tuesday – 4 x 1500m circuit (try to improve February's time by 5-10 sec), 3-4 min jog recovery between each; follow this with 3 miles easy run.
Wednesday – 8 miles easy steady-state run.
Thursday – 6 miles run split up: 4 miles fast; 1 mile easy; 1 mile fast.
Friday – rest day.
Saturday – first week: 6 x 1000m circuit, 30 sec recovery jog between each; 20 min rest; 15 min mobility exercises; 30min sprint drills.
Second week: cross-country race or 5k-10k road-race.
Sunday – 10 miles easy steady-state run.

The pre-track competition phase – 13 weeks

March Last two weeks **April**: first week
Monday – 6 miles medium steady-state run.
Tuesday – 5 x 600m circuit (pulse rate approximately 150/160 beats per minute), 1min recovery between each.
Wednesday – 5 miles run split up: 3 miles fast; 1 mile easy; 1 mile fast.
Thursday – track 8 x 300m (48sec), 300m jog between each; check that pulse rates are in the vicinity of 180 and 120 beats per minute; 20 min rest; follow this with 8 x 100m sprint – slow walk back between each 100m.
Friday – rest day.
Saturday – 5 mile fartlek; 20 min rest; 15 min mobility exercises; 30 min sprint drills.
Sunday – 10 miles easy steady-state run.

April Middle 3 weeks.
Monday – 5 miles fartlek.
Tuesday – track 3 x 600m (96sec), 400m jog between each; 20 min rest; 4 x 150m sprint; slow walk back between each.
Wednesday – 6 miles medium steady-state run.
Thursday – track 8 x 300m (45/46sec), 300m jog between each; 20 min rest; 6 x 100m fast relaxed strides; 100m jog between each.
Friday – rest day.
Saturday – 5 x 600m circuit (try to be about 2/3 sec faster than in previous 3 weeks), 1 min recovery jog between each; 20 min rest; 15 min mobility exercises; 30 min sprint drills.
Sunday – 10 miles easy steady-state run.
April Last week – (recuperation week).
Monday – 5 miles easy steady-state run.
Tuesday – 5 miles fartlek.
Wednesday – track 6 x 200m (30/31sec), 200m jog between each.
Thursday – 5 miles easy steady-state run.
Friday – rest day.
Saturday – track 6 x 100m sprint; 100m slow walk-back between each.
Sunday – 5 miles easy steady-state run.

May First 3 weeks.
Monday – 5 x 600m circuit, (maintain times of previous three weeks), 1 min recovery jog between each.
Tuesday – track 4 x 300m (42/43sec), 400m walk/jog between each; 20 min rest; 6 x 100m fast relaxed strides; 100m jog between each.
Wednesday – 5 miles medium steady-state run.
Thursday – track 4 x 500m (76/77sec), 300m jog between each; 20 min rest; 3 x 150m sprint; 150m slow walk back between each.
Friday – rest day.
Saturday – track 1 x 1000m (aim for 2min 40sec),

8min walk/jog; 3 x 200m (29/30secs), 200m jog between each, 20 min rest; 15 min mobility exercises; 30 min sprint drills.
Sunday – 8 miles easy steady-state run.

Track competition phase
2 week cycle for training between 800m races.

Day 1	4 x 1000m circuit (medium/hard), 2 min recovery between each; 20 min rest; 6 x 100m fast relaxed strides; 100m slow walk back between each.
Day 2	6 x 200m fast (26/27sec), 200m jog between each; 10 min rest; 4 miles easy steady-state run.
Day 3	6 x 300m (43/44sec), 300m jog between each; 20 min rest; 15/20 min mobility exercises.
Day 4	5 miles medium steady-state run.
Day 5	3 x 500m (75/76sec) 7-8 min recovery between each; 20 min rest; 6 x 50m sprint. Slow walk back between each.
Day 6	rest day.
Day 7	2 x 900m split up: 300m steady (50sec), 300m fast (46/47sec), 300m steady (50sec), 10 min rest between each 900m; 20 min rest; 15 min mobility exercises; 20 min sprint drills.
Day 8	8 miles easy steady-state run.
Day 9	1 x 1000m (2min/40sec) 10 min rest; 1 x 600m (96sec) 10min rest; 3 x 100m fast stride, 100m jog between each.
Day 10	5 miles Fartlek.
Day 11	6 x 200m relaxed (28/29sec), 200m jog between each; 15 min mobility exercises.
Day 12	5 miles easy steady-state run.
Day 13	rest day.
Day 14	800m race.

May Last week. **June** first two weeks.
Monday – 5 miles Fartlek.
Tuesday – 4 x 400m split: 200m steady (32sec), 200m fast (28sec), 400m walk/jog between each; 20 min rest; 6 x 100m sprint, slow walk back between each.
Wednesday – 6 miles medium steady-state run.
Thursday – 2 x 1000m split: 500m fast (77/78sec), 200m jog, 300m fast (46/47sec), 10 min rest between each 1000m; 20 min rest; 15-20 min mobility exercises; follow this with 3 x 150m fast relaxed strides; 150m walk between each.
Friday – rest day.
Saturday – 3 sets 3 x 200m (29/30sec), 100m jog between each 200m, 400m jog betwen each set; 20 min rest; 15-20 min mobility exercises; 30 min sprint drills; substitute a 1500m race for this session during the first week in June.
Sunday – 8 miles easy steady-state run.

800 metres
Schedules for a runner with a personal best of 1min 52sec, able to train twice each day. Aims to run cross-country at club level occasionally during the winter. Plans to have one high-level 800m race every 2 weeks during the summer and one low level 800m race or a race at another distance in the intervening week.

Endurance phase
October to mid-March – 24 weeks

October First two weeks – 5 miles easy steady-state run on Monday, Wednesday, Friday and Sunday.
October Second two weeks – 5 miles easy steady-state run on Monday, Tuesday, Thursday and Friday. 10 miles easy steady-state run on Sunday.
November Each week.

Monday	AM	5 miles easy steady-state run.
	PM	5 miles medium steady-state run.
Tuesday	PM	8 miles easy steady-state run.
Wednesday	AM	5 miles easy steady state run.
	PM	3 miles fast steady-state run.
Thursday	AM	5 miles easy steady-state run.
	PM	5 miles easy steady-state run.
Friday		rest day.
Saturday	PM	5 miles fast steady-state run.
Sunday	AM	10 miles easy steady-state run.

December First two weeks and last two weeks.

Monday	AM	5 miles easy steady-state run.
	PM	6 miles medium steady-state run.
Tuesday	AM	5 miles easy steady-state run.
	PM	4 x 1500m circuit (aim for 150/160 pulse rate), 2 min jog recovery between each.
Wednesday	PM	8 miles medium steady-state run.
Thursday	AM	5 miles easy steady-state run.
	PM	5 miles fast steady-state run.
Friday		rest day.
Saturday	AM	5 miles easy steady-state run.
	PM	6 x 1000m circuit (aim for 150/160 pulse rate), 1 min recovery jog between each; 20 min rest; 15 min mobility exercises; 30 min sprint drills.
Sunday	AM	10 miles easy steady-state run.

December Middle week (recuperation week) – 6 miles easy steady-state run on Monday, Tuesday, Thursday, Saturday and Sunday.

January First four weeks.

Monday	AM	5 miles easy steady-state run.
	PM	8 miles easy steady-state run.
Tuesday	AM	5 miles easy steady-state run.
	PM	4 x 1500m circuit (try to improve December times by 3-5sec), 2 min jog recovery between each.
Wednesday	AM	5 miles easy steady-state run.
	PM	7 miles run split up: 5 miles fast, 1 mile easy, 1 mile fast.
Thursday	AM	5 miles easy steady-state run.
	PM	track: 12 x 200m (29/30sec), 200m recovery jog between each.
Friday	AM	5 miles easy steady-state run.
Saturday	AM	5 miles easy steady-state run.
	PM	6 x 1000m circuit (try to maintain December's times but reduce recovery to 30sec between each repetition); 20 min rest; 15 min mobility exercises; 30 min sprint drills. On alternate weeks substitute a cross-country race
	PM	6 x 150m easy relaxed strides. Walk back slowly between each.

January Last week — 6 miles easy steady-state run on Monday, Tuesday, Thursday and Saturday. 4 miles easy steady-state run on Sunday plus 6 x 200m relaxed strides; 200m jog between each.

February Four weeks.

Monday	AM	6 miles easy steady-state run.
	PM	8 miles medium steady-state run.
Tuesday	AM	5 miles easy steady-state run.
	PM	4 x 1500m circuit (try to improve January's time by 2-3 sec); 3 min jog recovery between each.
Wednesday	AM	6 miles easy steady-state run.
	PM	7 miles run split up: 5 miles fast, 1 mile easy, 1 mile fast.
Thursday	AM	5 miles easy steady-state run.
	PM	track: 2 sets of 6 x 300m (44/45 sec); 300m jog between fast sections; 400m jog between sets.
Friday	AM	6 miles easy steady-state run.
Saturday	AM	5 miles easy steady-state run.
	PM	6 x 1000m circuit (try to improve January's time by 2-3 sec: 20 min rest; 15 min mobility exercises; 30 min sprint drills. On alternate weeks, substitute a cross-country race.
Sunday	AM	10 miles easy steady-state run.
	PM	5 miles Fartlek.

March First two weeks.

Monday	AM	5 miles easy steady-state run.
	PM	6 miles medium steady-state run.
Tuesday	AM	5 miles easy steady-state run.
	PM	4 x 1500m circuit (try to maintain February's times as relaxed as possible), 2 min recovery jog between each.
Wednesday	AM	5 miles easy steady-state run.
	PM	6 miles run split up: 4 miles fast, 1 mile easy, 1 mile fast.
Thursday	AM	5 miles easy steady-state run.
	PM	10 x 300m (44/45sec), 200m jog recovery between each; 20 min rest; 6 x 100m fast stride, 100m walk back between each.
Friday		rest day.
Saturday	AM	5 miles easy steady-state run.
	PM	5 x 1000m circuit (try to maintain February's times as relaxed as possible), 30 sec recovery jog between each. 20 min rest. 15 min mobility exercises. 30 min sprint drills. Alternate this with a cross-country race.
Sunday	AM	8 miles easy steady-state run.
	PM	5 miles Fartlek.

The pre-track competition phase – 13 weeks

March Last two weeks. **April** First week.

Monday	AM	5 miles medium steady-state run.
	PM	5 miles Fartlek.
Tuesday	AM	5 miles easy steady-state run.
	PM	4 x 400m (58sec), 300m jog recovery; 4 x 200m (28sec), 200m jog recovery.
Wednesday	AM	5 miles medium steady-state run.
	PM	6 miles run split up: 4 miles fast, 1 mile easy, 1 mile fast.
Thursday	AM	5 miles easy steady-state run.
	PM	track: 2 x 1000m (2min 30sec), 7-8 min recovery in between; 15 min rest: 4 x 150m split: 100m stride, 50m sprint, walk back slowly between each run.
Friday	AM	5 miles easy steady-state run.
Saturday	AM	5 miles easy steady-state run.
	PM	5 x 600m circuit (ensure pulse rate is in 150/160 range), 2 min recovery jog between each; 20 min rest: 15 min mobility exercises; 30 min sprint drills.
Sunday	AM	8 miles medium steady-state run.
	PM	4 miles easy steady-state run.

April Middle three weeks.

Monday	AM	5 miles medium-steady state run.
	PM	5 miles Fartlek.
Tuesday	AM	5 miles easy steady-state run.
	PM	4 x 400m (56/57sec), 300m jog recovery; 4 x 200m (27/28sec), 200m jog recovery.
Wednesday	AM	5 miles medium steady-state run.
	PM	5 miles Fartlek
Thursday	AM	5 miles easy steady-state run.
	PM	2 x 1000m (2min 27sec), 7-8 min recovery between each; 15 min rest: 4 x 150m split: 100m stride, 50m sprint (walk back slowly between each run).
Friday		rest day: just 15-20 min mobility exercises.
Saturday	AM	5 miles easy steady-state run.
	PM	5 x 600m (try to improve the previous 3 weeks' times by 2/3 sec), 2 min jog recovery between each; 20 min rest; 15 min mobility exercises; 30 min sprint drills.
Sunday	AM	8 miles medium steady-state run.
	PM	6 x 200m relaxed strides on grass, 200m jog recovery between each.

April Last week (recuperation week).

Monday	5 miles easy steady-state run.
Tuesday	5 miles Fartlek.
Wednesday	6 x 200m (29/30sec), 200m jog recovery between each.
Thursday	5 miles easy steady-state run.
Friday	rest day.
Saturday	6 x 100m sprint, 100m slow walk back between each.
Sunday	5 miles medium steady-state run.

May First three weeks.

Monday	AM	5 miles medium steady-state run.
	PM	4 x 400m (55/56sec), 400m jog recovery; 4 x 200m (26/27sec), 300m jog recovery.
Tuesday	AM	5 miles easy steady-state run.
	PM	5 miles Fartlek.
Wednesday	AM	20-30 min mobility exercises.
	PM	2 x 1000m (2min 25sec), 7-8 min recovery between each; 20 min rest; 4 x 150m split: 75m stride, 75m sprint (walk back slowly between each).
Thursday	AM	5 miles medium steady-state run.
	PM	4 sets 3 x 200m (28sec) 30 sec recovery between each 200m, 4 min recovery between sets; 20 min rest; 6 x 100m sprint, walk back slowly between each.
Friday		rest day.
Saturday	AM	5 miles easy steady-state run.
	PM	5 x 450/500m shallow hill (try to maintain normal length stride), jog down easily between each run; 20 min rest; 15 min mobility exercises; 30 min sprint drills. On the third week, substitute a 1500m race for this session.

May Last week. **June** First two weeks.

Monday AM 5 miles easy steady-state run.
PM 6 x 300m (40/41sec), 300m recovery jog between each; 20 min rest; 6 x 60m fast relaxed strides, (walk back slowly between each.

Tuesday AM 5 miles medium steady-state run.
PM 5 x 450/500m shallow hill (maintain technique, try to speed up recovery jog down slightly); 20 min rest; 15 min recovery exercises; 20 min sprint drills.

Wednesday AM 20-30 min mobility exercises.
PM 4 x 400m split up: 200m steady (28/29sec), 200m fast (26/27sec), 5/6 min recovery between each; 20 min rest; 4 x 60m fast relaxed strides, walk back slowly between each.

Thursday AM 5 miles medium steady-state run.
PM 4 sets 300m (40/41sec), 30 sec recovery 200m; (27/28sec), 5/6 minutes recovery between each.

Friday rest day.

Saturday AM 5 miles easy steady-state run.
PM 900m split up: 300m fast (41/42sec), 300m steady 45/46sec), 300m fast (41/42sec); 10 min recovery; 900m split up: 300m steady (45/46sec), 300m fast 41/42sec), 300m steady (45/46sec); 20 min rest; 15 min mobility exercises; 15 min sprint drills. In the middle week substitute a 400m or 1500m race for this session.

Sunday AM 8 miles easy steady-state run.
PM 4 miles easy steady-state run.

Track competition phase
2 weeks training between high quality races.

Day 1 AM 5 miles easy steady-state run.
PM 3 x 1000m circuit fast but relaxed, 4/5 min recovery jog between each; 20 min rest; 6 x 50m sprint, walk back slowly between each.

Day 2 AM 5 miles medium steady-state run.
PM 5 miles Fartlek.

Day 3 AM 15-20 min mobility exercises.
PM 800m split up: 600m fast (1min 22sec), 100m jog, 100m sprint, repeat twice with 10 min recovery between; 20 min rest; 3 x 150m split up: 100m stride, 50m sprint, slow walk back between each run.

Day 4 AM 5 miles easy steady-state run.
PM 6 x 300m relaxed intervals aim for 40/41sec as relaxed as possible), 300m jog recovery between each.

Day 5 rest day.

Day 6 low level 800m race or 400m or 1500m race.

Day 7 AM 6 miles easy steady-state run.
PM 6 x 100m fast relaxed strides on grass, walk back slowly between each.

Day 8 AM 5 miles easy steady-state run.
PM 2 x 400m fast (53/54sec), 7/8 min recovery between; 20 min rest; 3 x 150m split up: 100m stride, 50m sprint, walk back slowly between each.

Day 9 AM 15-20 min mobility exercises; 15-20 min sprint drills.

Day 10 AM 3 miles medium steady-state run.
PM 6 x 200m fast, relaxed strides, 200m recovery jog between each.

Day 11 AM 3 miles very easy run.
PM rest.

Day 12 rest day.

Day 13 high quality 800m race.

Day 14 AM 6 miles easy steady-state run.
PM 6 easy relaxed strides over 100m on grass, walk back slowly between each.

1500 metres

Schedules for a runner with a personal best of 4min 4sec, able to train once each day. Aims to race cross-country at club level occasionally during the winter and to race on the track once every two weeks in the summer.

Endurance phase
October to mid-March 24 weeks.

October First two weeks – 5 miles easy steady-state run on Monday, Wednesday, Friday and Sunday.
October Second two weeks – 5 miles easy steady-state run on Monday, Tuesday, Thursday and Friday. 10 miles easy steady-state run on Sunday.

November Each week – 5 miles easy steady-state run on Monday and Wednesday; 6 miles easy steady-state run on Tuesday and Thursday; 4 miles fast steady-state run on Saturday; 10 miles easy steady-state run on Sunday.

December First two weeks and last two weeks.

Monday	7 miles medium steady-state run.
Tuesday	5 miles fast steady-state run.
Wednesday	8 miles easy steady-state run.
Thursday	7 miles medium steady-state run.
Friday	rest day.
Saturday	6 x 1000m circuit (aim for 150/160 pulse rate), 1 min jog recovery between each; 20 min rest; 15 min mobility exercises; 30 min sprint drills.

December Middle week (recuperation week) – 5 miles easy steady-state run on Monday, Tuesday, Thursday, Friday and Sunday.

January First 4 weeks.

Monday	8 miles medium steady-state run.
Tuesday	6 miles run split up: 4 miles fast, 1 mile easy, 1 mile fast.
Wednesday	10 miles easy steady-state run.
Thursday	8 miles medium steady-state run.
Friday	rest day
Saturday	8 x 1000m circuit, 1 min jog recovery between each; 20 min rest; 15 min mobility exercises; 30 min sprint drills.
Sunday	10 miles easy steady-state run.

January Last week – 5 miles easy steady-state run on Monday, Tuesday, Thursday, Friday and Sunday.

February 4 weeks

Monday	8 miles medium steady-state run.
Tuesday	4 x 1500m circuit (aim for 150/160 pulse rate), 2 min jog recovery between each; follow this with 3 miles easy run.
Wednesday	10 miles easy steady-state run.
Thursday	8 miles run split up: 6 miles steady, 1 mile easy, 1 mile fast.
Friday	rest day.
Saturday	8 x 1000m circuit, 30sec recovery between each; 20 min rest; 15 min mobility exercises; 30 min sprint drills.

On alternate weeks, substitute a cross-country race, or 5k to 10k road-race for the above session.

Sunday	10 miles easy steady-state run.

March First 2 weeks.

Monday	6 miles medium steady-state run.
Tuesday	3 x 2000m circuit (aim for 150/160 pulse rate), 2-3 min jog recovery between each; follow this with 3 miles easy run.
Wednesday	8 miles easy steady-state run.
Thursday	6 miles run split up: 4 miles fast, 1 mile easy, 1 mile fast.
Friday	rest day.
Saturday	first week: 8 x 1000m circuit, 30 sec jog recovery between each; 20 min rest; 15 min mobility exercises; 30 min sprint drills. Second week: cross-country race or 5k to 10k road race.
Sunday	10 miles easy steady-state run.

The pre-track competition phase

March Last 2 weeks. **April** First week.

Monday	8 miles medium steady-state run.

Tuesday	5 miles Fartlek.
Wednesday	6 miles run split up: 4 miles steady, 1 mile easy, 1 mile fast.
Thursday	track: 8 x 400m (68sec), 300m jog between each (check that pulse rates are in the vicinity of 180 and 120 beats per minute); 20 min rest; 8 x 100m sprint, slow walk back between each.
Friday	rest day.
Saturday	6 x 1000m circuit (aim for times 2/4sec faster than Feb/March times), 2 min jog recovery between each; 20 min rest; 15 min mobility exercises; 30 min sprint drills.
Sunday	10 miles easy steady-state run.

April Middle 3 weeks.

Monday	8 miles medium steady-state run.
Tuesday	5 miles Fartlek.
Wednesday	6 miles run split up: 4 miles fast, 1 mile easy, 1 mile fast.
Thursday	8 x 400m (65/66sec), 300m jog between each; 20 min rest; 6 x 150m sprint, slow walk back between each.
Friday	rest day.
Saturday	6 x 1000m circuit (maintain previous period's times), $1\frac{1}{2}$ min jog recovery between each; 20 min rest. 15 min mobility exercises; 30 min sprint drills.
Sunday	10 miles easy steady-state run.

April Last week – recuperation week.

Monday	5 miles easy steady-state run.
Tuesday	5 miles Fartlek.
Wednesday	6 x 200m (31/32secs), 200m jog between each.
Thursday	5 miles easy steady-state run.
Friday	rest day.
Saturday	6 x 100m sprint, walk back slowly between each.
Sunday	5 miles easy steady-state run.

May First 3 weeks.

Monday	5 x 1000m circuit (maintain previous period's times), reduce recovery to one min jog.
Tuesday	6 x 400m (63/64sec), 400m jog between each; 20 min rest; 6 x 150m split up: 100m stride, 50m sprint, slow walk back between each.
Wednesday	6 miles medium steady-state run.
Thursday	4 x 600m (1min 40sec), 400m jog between each; 20 min rest; 15min mobility exercises; 6 x 100m fast relaxed strides, slow walk back between each.
Friday	rest day.
Saturday	1 x 2000m (aim for 5min 50sec), 8 min walk/jog recovery; 3 x 200m (32/33sec), 200m jog between each; 20 min rest; 15 min mobility exercises; 30 min sprint drills.
Sunday	8 miles steady-state run.

May Last week **June** First two weeks.

Monday	5 miles Fartlek.
Tuesday	4 x 600m split: 300m steady (53/54sec), 300m fast (47/48sec), 400m walk/jog between each; 6 x 100m fast relaxed strides, slow walk back between each.
Wednesday	6 miles medium steady-state run.
Thursday	2 x 1000m split up: 800m fast (2min 12sec), 100m jog, 100m sprint, 10 min recovery between each; 20 min rest; 3 x 150m split: 100m stride, 50m sprint, walk back slowly between each.
Friday	rest day.
Saturday	3 sets 4 x 200m (30/32sec), 100m jog between each 200m, 400m jog between sets; 20 min rest; 15/20 min mobility exercises; 30 min sprint drills. Substitute a 3000m race for this session during the first week in June.
Sunday	10 miles easy steady-state run.

Track competition phase
2 week cycle between 1500m races.

Day 1	4 x 1000m circuit (medium/hard), 2 min recovery between each; 20 min rest; 6 x 100m fast relaxed strides, slow walk back between each.
Day 2	5 miles Fartlek.
Day 3	6 x 300m fast (45/46sec), 300m jog between each; 20 min rest; 15-20 min mobility exercises.
Day 4	5 miles medium steady-state run.
Day 5	4 x 500m (78/80sec), 7-8 min recovery between each; 20 min rest; 6 x 50m sprint, slow walk back between each sprint.
Day 6	rest day.
Day 7	2 x 1200m split up: 400m steady (68/69sec); 400m fast (64/65sec); 400m steady (68/69sec), 10 min rest between each run; 20 min rest; 15 min mobility exercise; 20 min sprint drills.
Day 8	8 miles easy steady-state run.
Day 9	1 x 2000m (5min 40sec); 10 min rest; 1 x 1000m (2min 45sec); 10 min rest; 3 x 100m fast stride; 100m jog between each.
Day 10	5 miles Fartlek.
Day 11	6 x 200m relaxed (30/31sec), 200m jog between each; 15 min mobility exercises.
Day 12	easy 5 miles steady-state run.
Day 13	rest day.
Day 14	1500m race.

1500 metres

Schedules for a runner with a personal best of 3min 42sec able to train twice each day. Aims to race cross-country at a good level at the end of the Endurance phase. Plans to have one high level 1500m race every two weeks during the summer and to race at another distance in the intervening week.

Endurance phase
October to mid-March-24 weeks

October First 2 weeks. 5 miles easy steady-state run on Monday, Wednesday, Friday and Sunday.
October Second two weeks. 5 miles easy steady-state run on Monday, Tuesday, Thursday and Friday. 10 miles easy steady-state run on Sunday.

November Each week.

Monday	AM	5 miles easy steady-state run.
	PM	5 miles medium steady-state run.
Tuesday	PM	8 miles easy steady-state run.
Wednesday	AM	5 miles easy steady-state run.
	PM	3 miles fast steady-state run.
Thursday	AM	5 miles easy steady-state run.
	PM	5 miles medium steady-state run.
Friday		rest day.
Saturday	PM	5 miles fast steady-state run.
Sunday	AM	10 miles easy steady-state run.

December First two weeks and last two weeks.

Monday	AM	5 miles easy steady-state run.
	PM	6 miles medium steady-state run.
Tuesday	AM	5 miles easy steady-state run.
	PM	4 x 1500m circuit (aim for 150/160 pulse rate), 2 min recovery jog between each.
Wednesday	PM	8 miles medium steady-state run.
Thursday	AM	5 miles easy steady-state run.
	PM	5 miles fast steady-state run.
Friday		rest day.
Saturday	AM	5 miles easy steady-state run.
	PM	6 x 1000m circuit (aim for 150/160 pulse rate), 1 min recovery jog between each; 20 min rests; 15 min mobility exercise; 30 min sprint drills.
Sunday	AM	10 miles easy steady-state run.

December Middle week (recuperation week). 6 miles easy steady-state run on Monday, Tuesday, Thursday, Saturday and Sunday.

January First 4 weeks.

Monday	AM	5 miles easy steady-state run.
	PM	8 miles medium steady-state run.
Tuesday	AM	5 miles easy steady-state run.
	PM	5 x 1500m circuit (try to improve December's times by 2/3sec) 2 min recovery jog between each.
Wednesday	AM	5 miles easy steady-state run.
	PM	7 miles run split up: 5 miles fast, 1 mile easy, 1 mile fast.
Thursday	AM	5 miles easy steady-state run.
	PM	track 8 x 300m (46/47sec), 300m recovery jog between each.
Friday		5 miles easy steady-state run.
Saturday	AM	5 miles easy steady-state run.
	PM	6 x 1000m circuit (try to maintain December's times but reduce recovery to 30sec jog between each repetition); 20 min rest; 15 min mobility exercises; 30 min sprint drills.
Sunday	AM	10 miles easy steady-state run.
	PM	6 x 100m relaxed strides between each.

On alternative weeks substitute:

Thursday	AM	5 miles medium steady-state run.
	PM	5 miles easy steady-state run.
Friday		rest day.
Saturday		cross-country race.
Sunday	AM	8 miles easy steady-state run.
	PM	3 miles medium steady-state run.

January Last week (recuperation week). 6 miles easy steady-state run on Monday, Tuesday, Thursday and Saturday; 4 miles easy steady-state run on Sunday, plus 6 x 200m relaxed strides, 200m jog between each.

February Four weeks.

Monday	AM	6 miles easy steady-state run.
	PM	8 miles medium steady-state run.
Tuesday	AM	5 miles easy steady-state run.
	PM	4 x 2000m circuit (aim for 150/160 pulse rate), 2min recovery jog between each.
Wednesday	AM	6 miles easy steady-state run.
	PM	7 miles split up: 5 miles steady, 1 mile easy, 1 mile fast.
Thursday	AM	6 miles easy steady-state run.
	PM	track 8 x 400m (62/63sec), 300m jog recovery between each.

Friday	AM	5 miles easy steady-state run.
Saturday	AM	5 miles easy steady-state run.
	PM	8 x 1000m circuit (maintain December's times), 30sec recovery jog between each; 20 min rest; 15 min mobility exercises; 30 min sprint drills.
Sunday	AM	10 miles easy steady-state run.
	PM	4 miles easy steady-state run.

On alternative weeks substitute:

Wednesday	AM	4 miles easy steady-state run.
	PM	4 miles Fartlek.
Thursday	AM	5 miles easy steady-state run.
Friday		rest day.
Saturday		cross-country race.

March First 2 weeks.

Monday	AM	5 miles easy steady-state run.
	PM	7 miles medium steady-state run.
Tuesday	AM	5 miles easy steady-state run.
	PM	3 x 2000m circuit (aim for 4/5sec) faster than February's time), 3 min recovery jog between each.
Wednesday	AM	5 miles medium steady-state run.
	PM	6 miles run split up: 4 miles fast, 1 mile easy, 1 mile fast.
Thursday	AM	5 miles easy steady-state run.
	PM	8 x 400m (62/63sec), 200m recovery jog between each.
Friday	AM	5 miles easy steady-state run.
Saturday	AM	4 miles easy steady-state run.
	PM	6 x 1000m circuit (try to improve on February's time by 2/3sec), 2 min recovery jog between each; 20 min rest; 15 min mobility exercises; 30 minutes sprint drills.
Sunday	AM	10 miles easy steady-state run.
	PM	6 x 200m relaxed strides, 200m recovery jog between each.

On the second week substitute:

Wednesday	AM	4 miles easy steady-state run.
	PM	4 miles easy steady-state run.
Thursday	PM	4 miles easy steady-state run.
Friday		rest day.
Saturday		cross-country race.
Sunday	AM	8 miles easy steady-state run.
	PM	3 miles easy steady-state run.

The pre-track competition phase 13 weeks

March Last 2 weeks. **April** First week.

Monday	AM	5 miles medium steady-state run.
	PM	5 miles medium steady-state run.
Tuesday	AM	5 miles easy steady-state run.
	PM	5 x 800m (aim for 2min 6sec), 3 min recovery jog between each.
Wednesday	AM	5 miles easy steady-state run.
	PM	8 miles medium steady-state run.
Thursday	AM	5 miles easy steady-state run.
	PM	8 x 400m (61/62sec), 200m recovery jog between each; 15 min rest; 4 x 150m split: 100m stride, 50m sprint, walk back slowly between each run.
Friday	AM	5 miles easy steady-state run.
Saturday	AM	4 miles easy steady-state run.
	PM	4 x 2000m circuit (try to maintain previous period's times), reduce recovery to 90sec between each run; 20 min rest. 15 min mobility exercises; 30 min sprint drills.
Sunday	AM	10 miles easy steady-state run.
	PM	3 miles easy steady-state run.

April Middle three weeks.

Monday	AM	5 miles easy steady-state run.
	PM	5 miles medium steady-state run.
Tuesday	AM	5 miles easy steady-state run.
	PM	5 x 800m (aim for 2min 2sec), 4 min recovery jog between each; 20 min rest; 15 min mobility exercises; 6 x 60m sprint, walk back slowly between each.
Wednesday	PM	8 miles medium steady-state run.
Thursday	AM	5 miles easy steady-state run.
	PM	8 x 400m (60/61sec), 200m recovery jog between each; 20 min rest; 4 x 150m split: 100m stride, 50m sprint, walk back slowly between each run.
Friday	AM	5 miles easy steady-state run.
Saturday	AM	4 miles easy steady-state run.
	PM	3 x 2000m circuit (try to improve previous period's time by 4/5sec), 2 min recovery jog between each; 20 min rest; 15 min mobility exercises; 30 min sprint drills.
Sunday	AM	8 miles easy steady-state run.
	PM	4 miles Fartlek.

April Last week – recuperation week.

Monday	5 miles easy steady-state run.
Tuesday	5 miles Fartlek.
Wednesday	6 x 200m (29/30sec), 200m jog between each.
Thursday	5 miles easy steady-state run.
Friday	rest day.
Saturday	6 x 100m sprint, walk back slowly between each.
Sunday	5 miles easy steady-state run.

May First 3 weeks.

Monday	AM	5 miles easy steady-state run.
	PM	5 miles medium steady-state run.
Tuesday	AM	5 miles easy steady-state run.
	PM	8 x 400m (58/59sec), 400m recovery jog betwen each; 20 min rest; 4 x 150m split: 100m stride, 50m sprint, walk slowly between each run.
Wednesday	PM	8 miles medium steady-state run.
Thursday	AM	5 miles easy steady-state run.
	PM	1 x 2000m (aim for 5min 25sec), 8 min rest. 1 x 1000m (aim for 2min 36sec), 8 min rest; 2 x 300m (44/45sec), 300m recovery jog between each; 4 x 60m sprint, slow walk back between each; 15 min rest; 15 min mobility exercises.
Friday	AM	5 miles easy steady-state run.
Saturday	AM	4 miles easy steady-state run.
	PM	6 x 450/500m shallow hill (try to maintain normal length stride), jog down easy between each run; 20 min rest; 15 min mobility exercises; 20 min sprint drills. On the 3rd week substitute a 3000m race for this session.
Sunday	AM	8 miles easy steady-state run.
	PM	4 miles Fartlek.

May Last week. **June** First two weeks.

Monday	AM	5 miles easy steady-state run.
	PM	5 miles medium steady-state run.
Tuesday	AM	5 miles easy steady-state run.
	PM	6 x 400m (57/58sec), 100m walk, 300m jog between each; 20 min rest; 4 x 100m fast

relaxed strides, walk back slowly between each run.

Wednesday AM 8 miles medium steady-state run.

Thursday PM 5 sets 3 x 200m (28/29sec), 30sec recovery between each 200m; 4 min recovery between sets; 15 min rest; 15 min mobility exercises; 6 x 60m sprints, slow walk back between each.

Friday AM 3 miles easy run.

Saturday AM 4 miles easy steady-state run.
PM 2 x 1000m split up: 800m fast (2min), 100m jog, 100m sprint, 10 min recovery between each run; 20 min rest; 15 min mobility exercises; 20 min sprint drills. On the third week substitute a 3000m race for this session.

Sunday AM 8 miles easy steady-state run.
PM 3 miles Fartlek.

Track competition phase 14 days cycle between good quality 1500m races.

Day 1 AM 5 miles easy steady-state run.
PM 5 miles medium steady-state run.

Day 2 AM 5 miles easy steady-state run.
PM 6 x 400m (57/58sec) (try to maintain times as relaxed as possible), 400m jog between each; 20 min rest; 4 x 100m fast relaxed strides, walk back slowly between each.

Day 3 PM 6 miles medium steady-state run.

Day 4 AM 4 miles easy steady-state run.
PM 1000m split up: 400m fast (56sec), 200m steady (34sec), 400m fast (56sec), 10 min rest; 6 x 200m relaxed (28/29sec), 200m jog between each.

Day 5 AM 4 miles easy run.

Day 6 AM 2 miles easy run.
PM 800m race.

Day 7 AM 6 miles medium steady-state run.
PM 5 miles Fartlek.

Day 8 AM 4 miles easy steady-state run.
PM 3 x 500m fast (68sec), 7-8 min walk/jog recovery between each; 15 min rest; 4 x 100m relaxed strides, jog 100m between each.

Day 9 AM 4 miles easy steady-state run.
PM 6 x 300m relaxed (45/46sec), 300m jog recovery between each; 15 min mobility exercises; 15 min sprint drills.

Day 10 rest day.

Day 11 AM 4 miles easy run.
PM 6 x 100m relaxed strides, jog 100m between each.

Day 12 rest day.

Day 13 1500m race.

Day 14 AM 6 miles easy steady-state run.
PM 3 miles medium steady-state run.

5000 metres/10,000 metres

Schedules for runners with personal bests of 15min for 5000m or 31 min for 10,000m, able to train once each day. Aims to race cross-country every other week from January to mid-March. During the summer track season will aim to race at 5000m every other week and on 3-4 occasions to race at 10,000m.

Winter phase 24 weeks.

October First two weeks.
5 miles easy steady-state run on Monday, Tuesday, Thursday, Friday and Sunday.
October Last two weeks.
5 miles easy steady-state run on Monday, Thursday and Friday; 10 miles easy steady-state run on Tuesday and Thursday.

November Each week.

Monday	5 miles easy steady-state run.
Tuesday	10 miles easy steady-state run.
Wednesday	5 miles medium steady-state run.
Thursday	5 miles easy steady state run.
Friday	rest day.
Saturday	5 miles fast steady-state run.
Sunday	10 miles medium steady-state run.

December First 2 weeks.

Monday	6 miles easy steady-state run.
Tuesday	10 miles easy steady-state run.
Wednesday	8 miles run split up: 5 miles steady, 2 miles easy, 1 mile fast.
Thursday	6 miles easy steady-state run.
Friday	rest day.
Saturday	6 x 1500m circuit (aim for 150/160 pulse rate), 1 minute jog recovery between each.
Sunday	10 miles medium steady-state run.

December Middle week (recuperation week).
5 miles easy steady-state run on Monday, Tuesday, Thursday, Friday and Sunday.

December Last two weeks.

Monday	8 miles easy steady-state run.
Tuesday	10 miles easy steady-state run.
Wednesday	10 miles run split up: 6 miles steady, 2 miles easy, 2 miles fast.
Thursday	8 miles easy steady-state run.
Friday	rest day.
Saturday	6 x 1500m circuit (try to maintain times), reduce recovery to 30sec jog; 20 min rest; 15 min mobility exercises; 20 min sprint drills.
Sunday	12 miles medium steady-state run.

January First and 3rd week.

Monday	10 miles medium steady-state run.
Tuesday	10 miles easy steady-state run.
Wednesday	12 miles run split: 5 miles fast, 2 miles easy, 5 miles steady.
Thursday	10 miles medium steady-state run.
Friday	rest day.
Saturday	8 x 1500m circuit (maintain previous times), 1 min recovery jog between each; 20 min rest; 15 min mobility exercises; 20 min sprint drills.
Sunday	15 miles easy steady-state run.

January Second and 4th weeks.

Monday	10 miles medium steady-state run.
Tuesday	10 miles run split: 6 miles steady, 2 miles easy, 2 miles fast.
Wednesday	10 miles medium steady-state run.
Thursday	8 miles easy steady-state run.
Friday	rest day.
Saturday	cross-country race.
Sunday	12 miles easy steady-state run.

January Last week.
5 miles easy steady-state run on Monday, Tuesday, Thursday, Friday and Sunday.

February First and 3rd weeks.

Monday	7 miles fast steady-state run.
Tuesday	10 miles easy steady-state run.
Wednesday	10 miles run split up: 5 miles steady, 2 miles easy, 3 miles fast.
Thursday	10 miles medium steady-state run.

Friday	rest day.
Saturday	5 x 2000m circuit (aim for 150/160 pulse rate), 2 min recovery jog between each; 20 min rest; 15 min mobility exercises; 20 mins sprint drills.
Sunday	12 miles easy steady-state run.

February Second and 4th weeks.

Monday	8 miles medium steady-state run.
Tuesday	7 miles run split: 3 miles fast, 1 mile easy, 3 miles fast.
Wednesday	8 miles easy steady-state run.
Thursday	4 miles easy steady-state run.
Friday	rest day.
Saturday	cross-country race.
Sunday	10 miles easy steady-state run.

March First week.

Monday	6 miles fast steady-state run.
Tuesday	8 miles easy steady-state run.
Wednesday	7 miles run split: 3 miles fast, 1 mile easy, 1 mile fast.
Thursday	6 miles medium steady-state run.
Friday	rest day.
Saturday	5 x 2000m circuit (maintain February's time), reduce recovery jog to 1 min; 20 min rest; 15 min mobility exercises; 20 min sprint drills.
Sunday	12 miles easy steady-state run.

March Second week.

Monday	5 miles fast steady-state run.
Tuesday	6 miles easy steady-state run.
Wednesday	5 miles run split: 3 miles steady, 1 mile easy, 1 mile fast.
Thursday	3 miles easy steady-state run.
Friday	rest day.
Saturday	cross-country race.
Sunday	10 miles easy steady-state run.

Pre track competition phase 13 weeks

March Last 2 weeks. **April** First week.

Monday	8 miles medium steady-state run.
Tuesday	track 6 x 800m (2min 30sec), 2 min recovery jog between each; 10 min rest; 6 x 100m fast stride, slow walk back between each.
Wednesday	8 miles medium steady-state run.
Thursday	10 miles easy steady-state run.
Friday	rest day.
Saturday	5 x 2000m circuit (try to improve February's time by 4-5sec), maintain recovery jog at 2 min; 20 min rest; 15 min mobility exercises; 20 min sprint drills.
Sunday	12 miles easy steady-state run.

April Middle 3 weeks.

Monday	8 miles medium steady-state run.
Tuesday	track 6 x 800m (2min 25sec) 2 min recovery jog between each; 10 min rest; 6 x 150m fast stride, slow walk back between each.
Wednesday	8 miles medium steady-state run.
Thursday	5 miles Fartlek.
Friday	rest day.
Saturday	5 x 2000m circuit (maintain previous times), reduce recovery jog to 90sec; 20 min rest. 15 min mobility exercises; 20 min sprint drills.
Sunday	12 miles easy steady-state run.

April Last week (recuperation week).

Monday	4 miles easy steady-state run.
Tuesday	track 6 x 400m (72secs), 400m jog recovery between each.
Wednesday	rest day.
Thursday	5 miles medium steady-state run.
Friday	rest day.
Saturday	5 miles Fartlek.
Sunday	6 miles easy steady-state run.

May First 3 weeks.

Monday	8 miles medium steady-state run.
Tuesday	track 4 x 800m (2min 20sec), 3 min recovery jog between each; 10 min jog; 6 x 400m (67/68sec), 300m recovery jog between each; 10 min rest; 6 x 100m fast stride, walk back slowly between each.
Wednesday	6 miles easy steady-state run.
Thursday	5 miles Fartlek.
Friday	rest day.
Saturday	4 x 2000m circuit (try to improve previous period's time by 4-5 sec), 4-5 min walk/jog between each run; 20 min rest; 15 min mobility exercises; 20 min sprint drills.
Sunday	10 miles easy steady-state run.

During the first week in June substitute the following sessions:

Tuesday	track 4 x 800m (2min 18sec), 3-4 min jog recovery between each.
Wednesday	5 miles easy steady-state run.
Thursday	4 miles easy steady-state run.
Friday	rest day.
Saturday	10,000m race.
Sunday	3 miles easy steady-state run followed by 6 x 100m relaxed strides with 100m jog between each.

Track competition phase 14 day cycle between races.

Day 1	track 4 x 1200m (1st 400m steady – 74sec; 2nd 400m hard – 70sec; 3rd 400m steady – 74sec), 400m jog/walk between each repetition.
Day 2	6 miles easy steady-state run.
Day 3	track 12 x 400m (68/69sec), 200m jog recovery between each; 10 min rest; 6 x 100m relaxed stride, walk back slowly between each.
Day 4	6 miles medium steady-state run.
Day 5	rest day.
Day 6	2 x 3000m circuit (aim for 160/166 pulse rate), 4/5 minutes walk/jog recovery between each; 20 minutes rest; 15 min mobility exercises; 20 min sprint drills. On some occasions a 1500m or 3000m race can be substituted in place of this session.
Day 7	10 miles easy steady-state run.
Day 8	6 x 400m (67/68sec), 300m jog recovery between each.
Day 9	6 miles medium steady-state run.
Day 10	5 miles easy steady-state run.
Day 11	3 miles medium steady-state run.
Day 12	rest day.
Day 13	5000m race, alternate with 10,000m race.
Day 14	8 miles easy steady-state run.

5000m/10,000m schedules for runners with personal bests of 13min 30sec for 5000m, or 28min for 10,000m able to train twice each day. Aim to run well in major cross-country races in February and March. Will race at 3000m or 5000m once every two weeks and 10,000m once every 4 weeks.

Winter phase 24 weeks

October First two weeks.
5 miles easy steady-state run on Monday, Tuesday, Thursday, Friday and Sunday.

October Last 2 weeks.
5 miles easy steady-state run on Monday, Wednesday, Thursday and Friday. 10 miles easy steady-state run on Tuesday and Sunday.

November Each week.

Monday	AM	5 miles easy steady-state run.
	PM	5 miles medium steady-state run.
Tuesday	PM	10 miles medium steady-state run.
Wednesday	AM	5 miles easy steady-state run.
	PM	6 miles fast steady-state run.
Thursday	AM	5 miles easy steady-state run.
	PM	6 miles medium steady-state run.
Friday	AM	5 miles easy steady-state run.
Saturday	AM	5 miles easy steady-state run.
	PM	8 x 1000m circuit (aim for 150/160 pulse rate), 1 min recovery jog between each.
Sunday	AM	10 miles easy steady-state run.

December First two weeks.

Monday	AM	5 miles easy steady-state run.
	PM	6 miles medium steady-state run.
Tuesday	AM	10 miles medium steady-state run.
Wednesday	AM	5 miles easy steady-state run.
	PM	6 miles medium steady-state run.
Thursday	AM	5 miles easy steady-state run.
	PM	7 miles run split: 5 miles steady, 1 mile easy, 1 mile fast.
Friday	AM	5 miles easy steady-state run.
Saturday	PM	8 x 1000m circuit (maintain November's times), reduce recovery to 30 sec recovery jog between each; 20 min rest; 15 min mobility exercises; 20 min sprint drills.
Sunday	AM	12 miles easy steady-state run.

December Middle week (recuperation week).
5 miles easy steady-state run on Monday, Tuesday, Saturday and Sunday. 10 miles easy steady-state run on Thursday.

December Last 2 weeks.

Monday	AM	5 miles easy steady-state run.
	PM	6 miles medium steady-state run.
Tuesday	AM	5 miles easy steady-state run.
	PM	4 x 2000m circuit (aim for 150/160 pulse rate), 2 min recovery jog between each.
Wednesday	PM	10 miles easy steady-state run.
Thursday	AM	5 miles easy steady-state run.
	PM	8 miles run split: 4 miles steady, 1 mile easy, 3 miles fast.
Friday	AM	5 miles easy steady-state run.
Saturday	AM	5 miles easy steady-state run.
	PM	6 x 1500m circuit (aim for 150/160 pulse rate), 2 min recovery jog between each; 20 min rest; 15 min mobility exercises; 20 min sprint drills. Alternate this session with a cross-country race.
Sunday	AM	12 miles easy steady-state run.

January First 4 weeks.

Monday	AM	6 miles easy steady-state run.
	PM	8 miles medium steady-state run.
Tuesday	AM	6 miles easy steady-state run.
	PM	5 x 2000m circuit (maintain December's time), reduce recovery to 1 min jog.
Wednesday	AM	6 miles easy steady-state run.
	PM	10 miles medium steady-state run.
Thursday	AM	6 miles easy steady-state run.
	PM	10 miles run split: 6 miles steady, 1 mile easy, 3 miles fast.
Friday	AM	8 miles easy steady-state run.
Saturday	AM	6 miles easy steady-state run.
	PM	6 x 1500m circuit (try to improve on December's times by 3-4 sec), maintain recovery jog; 20 min rest; 15 minutes mobility exercises; 20 min sprint drills.

On the 2nd and 4th weeks substitute the following sessions:

Thursday	AM	6 miles easy steady-state run.
	PM	4 miles medium steady-state run.
Friday	AM	5 miles easy steady-state run.

Saturday AM 3 miles easy steady-state run.
PM cross-country race.

January Last week
(recuperation week).
5 miles easy steady-state run on Monday, Tuesday, Friday and Saturday; 10 miles easy steady-state run on Wednesday and Sunday.

February First and third week.

Monday	AM	5 miles easy steady-state run.
	PM	8 miles medium steady-state run.
Tuesday	AM	5 miles easy steady-state run.
	PM	4 x 2000m circuit (try to improve on January's time by 3-4 sec), maintain recovery jog at 1 min.
Wednesday	PM	10 miles easy steady-state run.
Thursday	AM	5 miles easy steady-state run.
	PM	7 miles run split: 5 miles steady, 1 mile easy, 1 mile fast.
Friday	AM	6 miles medium steady-state run.
Saturday	AM	5 miles easy steady-state run.
	PM	5 x 1500m circuit (maintain January's times), reduce recovery jog to 1 min; 20 min rest; 15 min mobility exercises; 20 min sprint drills.
Sunday	AM	10 miles medium steady-state run.
	PM	5 miles Fartlek.

February Second and 4th weeks.

Monday	AM	5 miles easy steady-state run.
	PM	6 miles medium steady-state run.
Tuesday	AM	5 miles easy steady-state run.
	PM	2 x 2000m, maintain previous weeks' times as relaxed as possible, recovery jog of 2 min between each run; follow with 3 miles easy run.
Wednesday	PM	8 miles medium steady-state run.
Thursday	PM	5 miles easy steady-state run.
Friday		rest day.
Saturday	AM	3 miles very easy run.
	PM	cross-country race.
Sunday	AM	8 miles easy steady-state run.
	PM	6 x 100m relaxed strides, walk back slowly between each.

March First week – similar to 1st week in February.

March 2nd week – similar to 2nd week in February.

Pre-track competition phase 13 weeks.

March Last 2 weeks **April** first week.

Monday	AM	5 miles easy steady-state run.
	PM	8 miles medium steady-state run.
Tuesday	AM	5 miles easy steady-state run.
	PM	track 6 x 800m (aim for 2min 12sec), 300m recovery jog between each; 6 x 200m (30/31 sec), 200m recovery jog between each.
Wednesday	PM	10 miles medium steady-state run.
Thursday	AM	5 miles easy steady-state run.
	PM	8 miles run split: 4 miles fast, 2 miles easy, 2 miles fast.
Friday	AM	6 miles easy steady-state run.
Saturday	AM	5 miles easy steady-state run.
	PM	6 x 1200m circuit (aim for 150/160 pulse rate), 2 min recovery jog between each; 20 min rest; 15 min mobility exercises; 20 min sprint drills.
Sunday	AM	10 miles medium steady-state run.
	PM	5 miles easy steady-state run.

April Middle 3 weeks.

Monday	AM	5 miles easy steady-state run.
	PM	8 miles medium steady-state run.
Tuesday	AM	5 miles easy steady-state run.
	PM	track 6 x 800m (aim for 2min 8sec), 300m recovery jog between each; 6 x 200m split: 150m stride, 50m sprint, 200m walk/jog between each.
Wednesday	PM	10 miles medium steady-state run.
Thursday	AM	5 miles easy steady-state run.
	PM	3 x 2000m circuit (aim for 150/160 pulse rate), 2 min recovery jog between each; 20 min rest; 15 min mobility exercises; 20 min sprint drills.
Friday	AM	6 miles easy steady-state run.

Saturday	AM	5 miles easy steady-state run.
	PM	track 4 x 1200m (aim for 3min 18sec), 400m jog between each.
Sunday	AM	10 miles easy steady-state run.
	PM	5 miles medium steady-state run.

April Last week (recuperation week).
5 miles easy steady-state run on Monday, Tuesday, Wednesday, Friday and Sunday; 5 miles Fartlek on Saturday.

May First 3 weeks.

Monday	AM	5 miles easy steady-state run.
	PM	8 miles medium steady-state run.
Tuesday	AM	5 miles easy steady-state run.
	PM	track 8 x 600m (aim for 93sec), 300m jog recovery between each; 4 x 200m split: 150m stride, 50m sprint, 200m walk/jog between each.
Wednesday	PM	10 miles easy steady-state run.
Thursday	AM	5 miles easy steady-state run.
	PM	8 miles run split: 3 miles fast, 2 miles easy, 3 miles fast.
Friday	AM	6 miles easy steady-state run.
Saturday	AM	3 miles easy steady-state run.
	PM	track 4 x 1200m (aim for 3min 12sec), 400m recovery jog between each; 20 min rest; 15 min mobility exercises; 20 min sprint drills.
Sunday	AM	10 miles easy steady-state run.
	PM	4 miles Fartlek.

May Last week. **June** First 2 weeks.

Monday	AM	5 miles easy steady-state run.
	PM	8 miles medium steady-state run.
Tuesday	AM	5 miles easy steady-state run.
	PM	track 5 sets of 3 x 400m (62sec), 30sec recovery jog between each 400m; 3 min recovery jog between each set; 15 min rest; 4 x 150m split: 100m stride, 50m sprint, walk/jog slowly back between each.
Wednesday	PM	10 miles medium steady-state run.
Thursday	AM	5 miles easy steady-state run.
	PM	6 miles Fartlek.
Friday	AM	4 miles easy steady-state run.
Saturday	AM	4 miles easy steady-state run.
	PM	track 4 x 1200m split: 1st 400m steady (65sec); 2nd 400m fast (60sec); 3rd 400m steady (65sec), 400m recovery jog between each.
Sunday	AM	10 miles medium steady-state run.
	PM	4 miles easy steady-state run.

For the first week in June substitute the following sessions:

Wednesday	PM	5 miles medium steady-state run.
Thursday	AM	5 miles easy steady-state run.
	PM	6 x 200m relaxed strides – 200m walk/jog between each.
Friday		rest day.
Saturday	AM	3 miles easy run.
	PM	1500m or 3000m race.
Sunday	AM	6 miles easy steady-state run.
	PM	4 miles Fartlek.

Track competition phase 14 day cycle between high quality races.

Day 1 AM 10 miles medium steady-state run.
PM 8 x 200m relaxed strides, 200m jog recovery.

Day 2 AM 3 miles easy run.
PM 1200m (attempt to run each 400m slightly faster than the one before eg. 67sec, 65sec, 63sec), 7-8 min recovery jog; 1200m: 1st lap 65sec, 2nd lap 60sec, 3rd lap 65sec, 7-8 min recovery jog; 1200m: 1st lap 62sec; 2nd lap 67sec; 3rd lap 62sec, 10 min rest; 4 x 100m relaxed strides, slow walk back between each.

Day 3 AM 5 miles easy steady-state run.
PM 5 miles medium steady-state run.

Day 4 AM 4 x 800m (aim for 2min 6sec as relaxed as possible), 400m jog recovery between each; 10 min rest; 4 x 200m split: 100m steady, 100m fast, 200m walk/jog between each.

Day 5 PM 8 miles medium steady-state run.

Day 6 AM 5 miles easy steady-state run.

Day 7 AM 3 miles easy run.
PM 1500m race or 2 x 2000m (aim for 160/170 pulse rate), 7-8 min jog recovery between; 10 min rest; 15 min mobility exercises; 20 min sprint drills.

Day 8 AM 10 miles medium steady-state run.
PM 5 miles easy steady-state run.

Day 9 PM 8 x 400m (aim for 60sec as relaxed as possible), 300m recovery jog between each; 4 x 150m split: 100m stride, 50m fast, slow walk back between each.

Day 10 AM 5 miles easy steady-state run.
PM 6 miles medium steady-state run.

Day 11 PM 5 miles medium steady-state run.

Day 12 rest day.

Day 13 AM 3 miles easy steady-state run.

Day 14 AM 3 miles easy steady-state run.
PM 3000m or 5000m race. If your main aim is 10,000m, try to fit in a race once every 4 weeks.

Schedule for 1500m runner wishing to compete in European Indoor and Outdoor track competition.
Is able to train twice each day and has personal best of 3min 42sec.

October First 2 weeks.
5 miles easy steady-state run on Monday, Tuesday, Thursday, Friday and Sunday.

October Last two weeks.
5 miles easy steady-state run on Monday and Thursday; 5 miles medium steady-state run on Tuesday and Friday; 10 miles easy steady-state run on Sunday.

November First 2 weeks.

Monday	AM	5 miles easy steady-state run.
	PM	6 miles medium steady-state run.
Tuesday	PM	6 x 1000m circuit (aim for 150/160 pulse rate), 2 min recovery jog in between.
Wednesday	PM	8 miles easy steady-state run.
Thursday	AM	3 miles easy steady-state run.
	PM	5 miles fast steady-state run.
Friday		rest day.
Saturday	AM	5 miles easy steady-state run.
	PM	5 miles Fartlek.
Sunday	AM	8 miles medium steady-state run.

November Second 2 weeks.

Monday	AM	5 miles easy steady-state run.
	PM	6 miles medium steady-state run.
Tuesday	AM	5 miles easy steady-state run.
	PM	6 x 1000m circuit (maintain previous times), reduce recovery to 1 min.
Wednesday	PM	8 miles medium steady-state run.
Thursday	AM	3 miles easy steady-state run.
	PM	7 miles run split: 5 miles steady, 1 mile easy, 1 mile fast.
Friday		rest day.
Saturday	AM	3 miles easy steady-state run.
	PM	Track 6 x 600m (aim for 96sec) 400m recovery jog between; 20 min rest; 15 min mobility exercises; 20 min sprint drills.
Sunday	AM	10 miles easy steady-state run.
	PM	6 x 100m relaxed strides, walk back slowly between each.

December First week (recuperation week).
5 miles easy steady-state run on Monday, Tuesday, Thursday and Sunday; 10 miles easy steady-state run on Wednesday.

Pre indoor competition phase – 8 weeks

December Middle 3 weeks.

Monday	AM	5 miles easy steady-state run.
	PM	6 miles medium steady-state run.
Tuesday	AM	5 miles easy steady-state run.
	PM	4 x 1200m circuit (aim for 150/160 pulse rate), 2 min recovery jog between each.
Wednesday	PM	8 miles medium steady-state run.
Thursday	AM	3 miles easy steady-state run.
	PM	6 x 600m (aim for 92/93sec) 400m recovery jog between; 10 min rest; 4 x 100m fast relaxed strides, walk back slowly between each.
Friday		rest day.
Saturday	AM	4 miles easy steady state run.
	PM	5 mile Fartlek.
Sunday	AM	10 miles easy steady-state run.
	PM	4 miles medium steady-state run.

December Last week. **January** First 3 weeks.

Monday	AM	5 miles easy steady-state run.
	PM	6 miles medium steady-state run.
Tuesday	AM	5 miles easy steady-state run.
	PM	3 x 1200m circuit (try to improve December times by 4-5sec) 2 min recovery jog between each; 10 min rest; 6 x 100m fast, relaxed strides, slow walk back between each.
Wednesday	PM	8 miles medium steady-state run.
Thursday	AM	3 miles easy steady-state run.
	PM	5 x 600m (aim for 89/90sec) 400m recovery jog between each; 10 min rest. 4 x 150m split: 100m stride, 50m sprint, walk back slowly between each.
Friday	AM	3 miles easy steady-state run.
Saturday	AM	4 miles easy steady-state run.
	PM	3 x 500m fast (aim at 67/68sec) 7-8 min walk/jog between each; 20 min rest; 15 min mobility exercises; 30 min sprint drills.
Sunday	AM	8 miles medium steady-state run.
	PM	4 miles easy steady-state run.

January Fourth week (recuperation week).
Easy 5 miles steady-state run on Monday and Wednesday; 8 miles easy steady state run on Sunday; 8 x 200m (29/30sec), with 200m jog between each on Tuesday; 5 miles Fartlek on Saturday.

January Last week.
Similar to first 3 weeks in January except that on Thursday you substitute:
AM 4 miles easy steady-state run.
PM 1 x 1000m (aim for 2min 30sec) 8 min rest, 3 x 400m split: 200m steady (30sec), 200m fast (27sec), 400m walk/jog recovery between each; 4 x 100m fast relaxed strides, slow walk back between each.

Indoor competition phase 7-8 weeks – 14 days training cycle

Day 1	AM	4 miles easy steady-state run.
	PM	2 x 600m (aim for 84/85sec) 8 min walk/jog recovery between; 3 x 200m fast (25/26sec), 200m walk/jog between each.
Day 2	AM	4 miles medium steady-state run.
	PM	5 miles Fartlek.
Day 3	AM	4 miles medium steady-state run.
	PM	4 x 300m split 150m steady 150m fast, 400m jog recovery between each; 10 min rest; 15 min mobility exercises; 20 min sprint drills.
Day 4	AM	4 miles easy steady-state run.
	PM	6 miles medium steady-state run.
Day 5		rest day.
Day 6		800m race.
Day 7	AM	8 miles easy steady-state run.
	PM	6 x 100m relaxed strides, walk back slowly between each.
Day 8	AM	4 miles easy steady-state run.
	PM	2 x 1000m (aim for 2min 30sec), 8 min walk/jog between each; 10 min rest; 3 x 400m (58sec as relaxed as possible), 400m jog between each.
Day 9	AM	4 miles easy steady-state run.
	PM	5 miles medium steady-state run.
Day 10	AM	4 miles easy steady-state run.
	PM	6 x 200m fast, but relaxed, 200m jog recovery between each.
Day 11		rest day.
Day 12		4 miles easy run.
Day 13		1500m race.
Day 14	AM	6 miles easy steady-state run.
	PM	6 x 100m relaxed strides, walk back slowly between each.

Endurance phase 5 weeks

March Last 2 weeks.
Use similar schedule to 2nd 2 weeks in November.

April First week (recuperation week).
Use similar schedule to 4th week in January.

April Middle 2 weeks.
Use similar schedule to 2nd 2 weeks in November.

Pre-outdoor competition phase 8 weeks

Middle April to early June
Use similar schedules to Pre-indoor Competition Phase.

Outdoor competition phase

Weeks 1-4	Use the 14 days cycle suggested for the indoor competition period.
Week 5	Use the recuperation schedule similar to the 4th week in January.
Weeks 6 & 7	Use the 14 days competition cycle
Week 8	Use the endurance schedule similar to the first week in November.
Weeks 9 & 10	Use the 14 days competition cycle.
Week 11	Use the recuperation week cycle.
Weeks 12 & 13	Use the 14 days competition cycle.

Schedules for a 1500m runner involved in the **North American College Competition Programme**. The runner has a personal best of 3min 48sec and is able to train twice each day. He is required to show good form at the peak of the cross-country season and will be expected to do well at the NCAAA indoor and outdoor track championships.

Endurance phase combined with cross-country season – 14 weeks.

September First 2 weeks.
5 miles easy steady-state run on Monday, Tuesday, Thursday and Friday; 10 miles easy steady-state run on Sunday.

September Second 2 weeks
5 miles easy steady-state run on Monday, Wednesday and Saturday; 5 miles medium steady-state run on Tuesday and Thursday; 10 miles medium steady-state run on Sunday.

October First 2 weeks

Monday	AM	5 miles easy steady-state run.
	PM	5 miles medium steady-state run.
Tuesday	PM	6 x 1200m circuit (aim for 150/160 pulse rate) 2 min recovery jog between each.
Wednesday	AM	5 miles easy steady-state run.
	PM	6 miles run split: 4 miles fast, 1 mile easy, 1 mile fast.
Thursday	PM	8 miles medium steady-state run.
Friday		rest day.
Saturday	AM	4 miles easy.
	PM	5 miles Fartlek or cross-country race.

October Fourth week **November** 1st 2 weeks.

Monday	AM	5 miles easy steady-state run.
	PM	6 miles medium steady-state run.
Tuesday	AM	5 miles easy steady-state run.
	PM	6 x 1200m circuit (try to improve October's times by 3-4sec), maintain recovery jog at 2 minutes.
Wednesday	PM	8 miles medium steady-state run.
Thursday	AM	5 miles easy steady-state run.
	PM	7 miles run split: 3 miles steady, 1 mile easy, 3 miles fast.
Friday		rest day.
Saturday	AM	4 miles easy steady-state run.
	PM	5 miles Fartlek or cross-country race.
Friday	AM	8 miles easy steady-state run.
	PM	12 x 200m relaxed stride, 200m jog between each.

November Third week semi-recuperation week.
5 miles easy steady-state run on Monday, Wednesday and Thursday; 10 miles easy steady-state run on Sunday; 5 miles Fartlek or cross-country race on Saturday.

November Last week **December** First 2 weeks.

Monday	AM	5 miles easy steady-state run.
	PM	6 x 500m shallow hill (try to maintain normal stride length)

		jog down quickly between each; repetition; 20 min rest; 15 min mobility exercises; 15 min sprint drills.
Tuesday	PM	8 miles medium steady-state run.
Wednesday	AM	5 miles easy steady-state run.
	PM	6 x 1000m circuit (aim for 150/160 pulse rate), 1 min recovery jog between each.
Thursday	AM	4 miles easy steady-state run.
	PM	4 miles medium steady-state run.
Friday		rest day.
Saturday	AM	3 miles easy steady-state run.
	PM	Cross-country race or 5 miles Fartlek.
Sunday	AM	8 miles easy steady-state run.
	PM	8 x 200m relaxed strides, 200m jog between each.

Pre-indoor competition phase – 6 weeks

December Last 3 weeks.

Monday	AM	5 miles easy steady-state run.
	PM	6 x 500m shallow hill (try to improve on November's times by 2-3sec), maintain good technique jog down slowly between each run.
Tuesday	PM	8 miles medium steady-state run.
Wednesday	AM	5 miles easy steady-state run.
	PM	8 x 400m (62sec) 300m jog recovery between each; 4 x 200m split: 100m stride, 100m sprint, walk/jog 200m between each.
Thursday	AM	5 miles medium steady-state run.
	PM	5 miles Fartlek.
Friday		rest day.
Saturday	AM	4 miles easy steady-state run.
	PM	4 x 1000m circuit (try to improve November's times by 3-4sec), 2 min recovery jog between each; 20 min rest; 15 min mobility exercise; 30 min sprint drills.
Sunday	AM	8 miles medium steady-state run.
	PM	6 x 200m relaxed strides, 200m jog between each.

January First week semi-recuperation week.

Monday	AM	5 miles medium steady-state run.
Tuesday	PM	6 x 400m (61-62sec) 300m jog between each.
Wednesday		rest day
Thursday	PM	6 miles medium steady-state run.
Friday	PM	5 miles easy steady-state run.
Saturday		rest day.
Sunday	PM	12 x 200m (29-30sec), 200m recovery jog between each.

Janauary Second and 3rd weeks.

Monday	AM	5 miles easy steady-state run.
	PM	6 miles run split: 4 miles steady, 1 mile easy, 1 mile fast.
Tuesday	AM	5 miles easy steady-state run.
	PM	8 x 400m (59-60sec) 300m recovery jog between each; 6 x 150m split: 100m stride, 50m sprint, slowly jog back between each.
Wednesday	PM	6 miles medium steady-state run.
Thursday	AM	5 miles easy steady-state run.
	PM	4 sets 3 x 200m (29-30sec) 30sec recovery between each 200m. 6-7 min recovery between sets. 10 min rest. 3 sets 3 x 100m sprint. 30sec recovery between each 100m. 6-7 min between each set.
Friday		rest day.
Saturday	AM	3 miles easy steady-state run.
	PM	track – 1 x 1000m (aim for 2min 36sec) 10 min recovery. 3 x 300m (41-42sec) 400m recovery jog between each; 10 min recovery; 6 x 50m sprint, slow walk back between each.
Sunday	AM	8 miles medium steady state run.
	PM	8 x 200m relaxed strides, 200m jog between each.

Indoor competition period – 8 weeks 2 week cycle between important races.

Day 1	AM	5 miles easy steady-state run.
	PM	3 x 500m fast (70sec) 400m recovery jog between each; 10min rest; 15 min mobility exercise; 3 x 150m split: 100m steady, 50m fast, slow walk back between each.
Day 2	PM	6 miles medium steady-state run.
Day 3	AM	4 miles easy steady-state run.
	PM	6 x 400m (aim for 60secs as relaxed as possible), 300m recovery jog between each; 10 min rest, 15 min mobility exercise; 15 min sprint drills.
Day 4	AM	4 miles easy steady-state run.
	PM	5 miles medium steady-state run.
Day 5		rest day.
Day 6	PM	800m or 3000m race, or 4 x 800m (2min 3sec) 400m recovery jog between each.
Day 7	AM	8 miles easy steady-state run.
	PM	6 x 200m relaxed strides. 200m jog back in between.
Day 8	PM	1 x 1000m (aim for 2min 30sec), 10 min recovery. 2 x 400m (58-59sec), 400m recovery jog between; 6 x 50m sprint, slow walk back between each.
Day 9	AM	3 miles easy steady-state run.
	PM	3 miles easy steady-state run.
Day 10	PM	6 x 200m relaxed strides, 200m walk/jog between each.
Day 11	AM	3 miles easy steady-state run.
Day 12		rest day.
Day 13		1500m race.
Day 14	AM	6 miles easy steady-state run.
	PM	3 miles easy steady-state run.

Pre-outdoor competition phase – 3 weeks

March – 5 miles easy steady-state run on Monday and Wednesday, 5 miles medium steady-state run on Tuesday and Thursday. 6 x 1000m circuit relaxed on Saturday, 2 min jog recovery between each, 8 miles medium steady-state run on Sunday.

March Third and 4th weeks.

Monday	AM	5 miles easy steady-state run.
	PM	6 miles medium steady-state run.
Tuesday	PM	4 x 1200m circuit (aim for 150/160 pulse rate), 2 min recovery jog between each.
Wednesday	AM	5 miles easy steady-state run.
	PM	8 miles medium steady-state run.
Thursday	AM	4 miles easy steady-state run.
	PM	5 miles fast steady-state run.
Friday		rest day.
Saturday	AM	4 miles easy steady-state run.
	PM	track 4 x 800m (2min 3sec), 400m recovery jog between each; 10 min rest; 15 min mobility exercise. 20 min sprint drills.
Sunday	AM	10 miles easy steady-state run.
	PM	6 x 200m relaxed strides, 200m jog between each.

Outdoor track competition phase – 12 weeks
Use the 14 days cycle suggested for the indoor competition period.

CHAPTER SEVEN

ROAD RUNNING

(including the Marathon)

One chapter cannot possibly cover every aspect of the wide range of events that are included under this heading, but I hope that I can make some points that will help those of you who race on the roads.

No doubt you will appreciate that for distances over 10 kilometres, it is mainly improvement of the aerobic energy system that will bring about better performances and your long-term plan will be to build up the distance gradually and increase the pace of your aerobic runs. The top ranks of the longer distance events are gradually becoming dominated by athletes who have very good under-distance performances, which brings home the point that it is not just the distance covered that is important, but the pace involved is just as vital. The so-called fast runners do not really possess great speed; many would have some difficulty in running a fast 400m. What they have developed is the ability to take up maximum oxygen when running at a faster pace than the slower runners. I would like to see prospective road-runners concentrate for a while on producing good 5000m and 10,000m results and then have another period bringing down their times for road races over 10, 15 and 20 miles before eventually tackling the marathon.

This was the approach adopted by one of the runners I coached, Tony Simmons, an athlete who ran for Great Britain at all distances from 1500m to the marathon. Tony, who was 4th in the 1976 Olympic 10,000m, probably trained less than most marathon runners yet recorded 2hr 12min. Tony was picking up maximum oxygen at just under 5-minute mile pace and his constant aim in training was to extend the distance for holding the pace. This pace felt comfortable to him, so it seemed logical to attempt to maintain the pace for the whole 26 miles. On the other hand, I coach two women, Margaret Lockley who has a best of 2hr 36min, and Rosemary Ellis (2hr 41min), neither of whom possessed any under-distance pedigree, so their problem was quite different. Their forte lay in their endurance so they ran more miles than Tony but also spent periods trying specifically to reduce their under-distance times.

Thus the long-distance runner, in the main, has the problem of varying the pace and distance of steady-state runs and juggling with the pace, number and recovery times of aerobic repetition sessions. Although training for 10 kilometres upwards is predominantly aerobic running, I think it is important to include some lactic anaerobic work to combat such occurrences as over-fast starts, uphill sections and fast surges.

Road runners should not neglect mobility exercises as an easy moving body requires less energy. I would place specific emphasis on back exercises as this area takes a lot of pounding during the many miles of running that are required. Conservation of energy is even more important in the longer distances so an efficient and economical technique is a valuable asset. A small amount of time spent regularly on developing leg strength will be valuable, too. These exercises could help you greatly in your attempts to maintain a decent stride-length, especially when you become very tired, either uphill or during the closing stages of a long race.

Training plans

Planning your training for road races is just as important as the planning for track races, and you should be quite clear in your mind what you are trying to achieve. Is it to be a 10 mile race every other week or a marathon two or three times a year? Once again, I must stress that the object of training is to produce good race results. You do not want to be training like a demon and racing badly. If you are going to race frequently over the shorter road-races i.e. 5 miles to 15 miles, then I would suggest that you vary the distances and the quality of the races. Select a few races that are particularly important to you and use the in-between races as build-ups. I suggest

Road running over a whole range of distances is becoming increasingly popular with athletes of all abilities. Steve Anders, Steve Harris and Dave Lewis (above) and Angela and Susan Toobey, Kirsty Wade and Christine Benning (right) all race regularly on the road

that you use the 10,000m schedules during the Winter phase and then adopt the following 14-day cycle for the Spring and Summer periods:-

14 day cycle between road races for runners able to train twice each day.

Day 1	AM	15 mile easy steady-state run.
	PM	3 miles Fartlek.
Day 2	AM	5 miles easy steady-state run.
	PM	8 miles medium steady-state run.
Day 3	AM	5 miles easy steady-state run.
	PM	6 x 1500m circuit (aim for 150/160 pulse rate); 1 minute recovery jog between each; 5 miles easy steady-state.
Day 4	PM	6 miles fast steady-state run.
Day 5		rest day.
Day 6	AM	5 miles easy steady-state run.
	PM	4 x 3000m circuit (aim for 150/160 pulse rate), 2min recovery jog between each.
Day 7	AM	12 miles easy steady-state run.
	PM	8 x 200m relaxed strides; 200m jog between each.
Day 8	AM	5 miles easy steady-state run.
	PM	8 x 500m shallow hill (try to maintain normal stride length); quick jog down between each repetition.
Day 9	PM	10 miles medium steady-state run.
Day 10	AM	3miles easy steady-state run.
	PM	7 miles run split: 5 miles fast, 1 mile easy, 1 mile fast.
Day 11	PM	4 miles easy steady-state run.
Day 12		rest day.
Day 13		road race.
Day 11	AM	5 miles easy steady-state run.
	PM	3 miles easy steady-state run.

I would also include 20 minutes of mobility exercises twice each week.

The New York Marathon was the first big city marathon to attract a mass international field. Here, runners cross the Verrazano Bridge

Training for the Marathon

If you are planning to race at the marathon distance you must bear in mind that it is asking a great deal for the chemical factory that we call a body to keep working at full output for two to three hours. Gradually keep extending the distance you can handle a certain pace, and your body will soon adapt to this treatment. Alternatively, gradually keep increasing the pace of some of your shorter steady-state runs. In this way you are improving your output, both in quality and quantity. In time your oxygen uptake will get better and the speed at which you are pulling out maximum oxygen will also improve. When this starts to happen you will find that you can record faster times for certain distances with less effort than before. To continue the analogy with the chemical factory – such an organization profits when it maintains costs and increases production. But have no illusions: there is no easy way to run a fast marathon and your training must be so comprehensive as to almost guarantee not just covering the distance, but completing it in a reasonable time. This is why I recommend occasionally running over-distance, i.e. 28 or 30 miles. This is to give you the confidence that comes with knowing that your body can operate for that length of time. Again, I suggest that would-be marathon runners follow the Winter schedules set out for 10,000m runners. After that I suggest a 3-month build up similar to the one that follows:

3-month preparation for a marathon race

Mileage chart

	Month 1	Month 2	Month 3
Week 1	80 miles	84 miles	77 miles
Week 2	96 miles	107 miles	92 miles
Week 3	63 miles	63 miles	65 miles
Week 4	75 miles	80 miles	75 miles

Training

Note: s.s.r. (steady-state run)

Month 1

Week 1

Day 1 AM 10 miles medium s.s.r.
PM 5 miles easy s.s.r.
Day 2 AM 6 miles medium s.s.r.
PM 8 x 1200m circuit (aim for 150/160 pulse rate); 2min jog recovery between each.
Day 3 AM 5 miles easy s.s.r.
PM 8 miles medium s.s.r.
Day 4 PM 10 miles medium s.s.r.
Day 5 AM 5 miles easy s.s.r.
PM 8 miles medium s.s.r.
Day 6 AM 5 miles easy s.s.r.
Day 7 AM 5 miles easy s.s.r.
PM 8 miles fast s.s.r.

Week 2

Day 1 AM 15 miles medium s.s.r.
PM 5 miles easy s.s.r.
Day 2 AM 7 miles medium s.s.r.
PM 4 x 2 miles circuit (aim for 150/160 pulse rate); 2min jog recovery between each.
Day 3 AM 7 miles easy s.s.r.
PM 7 miles medium s.s.r.
Day 4 AM 10 miles medium s.s.r.
Day 5 AM 5 miles easy s.s.r.
PM 6 miles fast s.s.r.
Day 6 rest day.
Day 7 AM 25 miles easy s.s.r.

Week 3

Day 1 AM 5 miles easy s.s.r.
PM 5 miles Fartlek.
Day 2 AM 10 miles easy s.s.r.
Day 3 AM 5 miles easy s.s.r.
PM 8 miles medium s.s.r.
Day 4 AM 5 miles easy s.s.r.
Day 5 PM 10 miles medium s.s.r.
Day 6 AM 5 miles easy s.s.r.
Day 7 AM 5 miles easy s.s.r.
PM 8 x 1200m (maintain week 1 times) reduce recovery jog to 1min.

Week 4

Day 1 AM 12 miles medium s.s.r.
PM 4 miles easy s.s.r.
Day 2 AM 5 miles medium s.s.r.
PM 6 miles fast s.s.r.
Day 3 AM 5 miles easy s.s.r.
PM 5 miles Fartlek.
Day 4 PM 10 miles medium s.s.r.
Day 5 AM 5 miles easy s.s.r.
PM 5 miles medium s.s.r.
Day 6 AM 3 miles easy s.s.r.
Day 7 PM 15 miles race.

Month 2

Week 1

Day 1 AM 10 miles medium s.s.r.
PM 5 miles easy s.s.r.
Day 2 AM 6 miles medium s.s.r.
PM 8 x 1200m circuit (maintain previous times) reduce recovery jog to 30sec.
Day 3 AM 5 miles easy s.s.r.
PM 8 miles medium s.s.r.
Day 4 PM 12 miles medium s.s.r.
Day 5 AM 5 miles easy s.s.r.
PM 8 miles medium s.s.r.
Day 6 PM 5 miles easy s.s.r.
Day 7 AM 5 miles medium s.s.r.
PM 10 miles fast s.s.r.

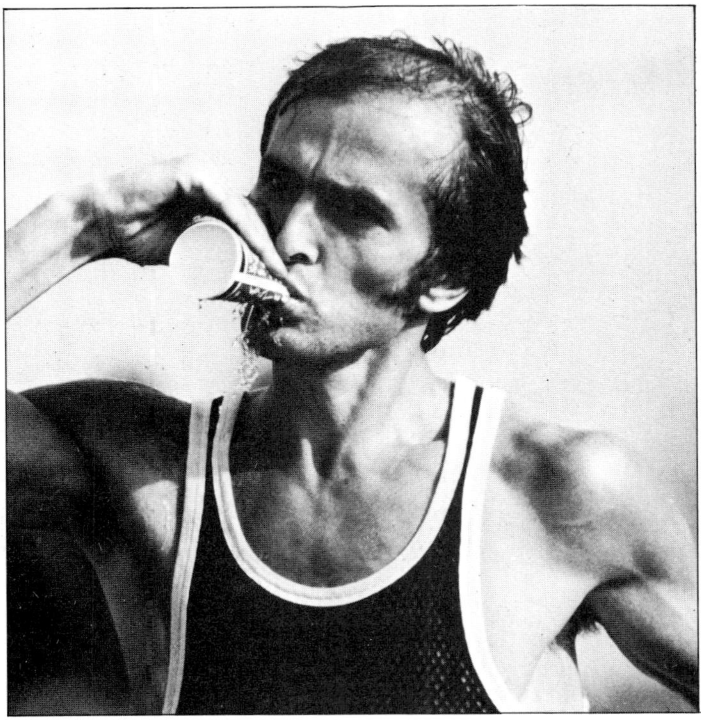

The Polytechnic Marathon(top), which started at Windsor Castle, was Britain's oldest Marathon. It is important to drink (left and above) to replace water and body salts lost through perspiration

Week 2

Day 1	AM	15 miles easy s.s.r.
	PM	5 miles medium s.s.r.
Day 2	AM	7 miles easy s.s.r.
	PM	4 x 3 miles circuit (aim for 150/160 pulse rate); 2min recovery jog between each.
Day 3	AM	7 miles easy s.s.r.
	PM	7 miles medium s.s.r.
Day 4	PM	12 miles medium s.s.r.
Day 5	AM	5 miles easy s.s.r.
	PM	6 miles fast s.s.r.
Day 6		rest day.
Day 7	AM	30 miles easy s.s.r.

Week 3

Day 1	AM	5 miles easy s.s.r.
	PM	5 miles easy s.s.r.
Day 2	PM	8 miles easy s.s.r.
Day 3	AM	5 miles easy s.s.r.
	PM	8 miles medium s.s.r.
Day 4	PM	5 miles easy s.s.r.
Day 5	PM	10 miles mediums.s.r.
Day 6	PM	5 miles easy s.s.r.
Day 7	AM	5 miles easy s.s.r.
	PM	8 x 1200m circuit (maintain) times) maintain recovery jog.

Week 4

Day 1	AM	12 miles medium s.s.r.
	PM	4 miles easy s.s.r.
Day 2	AM	5 miles medium s.s.r.
	PM	6 miles fast s.s.r.
Day 3	AM	5 miles easy s.s.r.
	PM	5 miles Fartlek.
Day 4	PM	10 miles medium s.s.r.
Day 5	AM	5 miles easy s.s.r.
	PM	5 miles easy s.s.r.
Day 6	AM	3 miles easy s.s.r.
Day 7	PM	20 miles race.

Month 3

Week 1

Day 1	AM	10 miles easy s.s.r.
Day 2	AM	5 miles easy s.s.r.
	PM	5 miles easy s.s.r.
Day 3	PM	12 miles medium s.s.r.
Day 4	AM	6 miles easy s.s.r.
	PM	8 x 1200m circuit (try to improve previous times by 4-6sec); 1min jog recovery between each.
Day 5	AM	5 miles easy s.s.r.
	PM	8 miles medium s.s.r.
Day 6	AM	5 miles easy s.s.r.
Day 7	AM	5 miles medium s.s.r.
	PM	8 miles fast s.s.r.

Week 2

Day 1	AM	15 miles easy s.s.r.
	PM	5 miles medium s.s.r.
Day 2	AM	7 miles medium s.s.r.
	PM	4 x 3 miles circuit (try to improve on previous times by 10-15sec) maintain recovery jog at 2min.
Day 3	AM	7 miles easy s.s.r.
	PM	7 miles medium s.s.r.
Day 4	PM	12 miles medium s.s.r.
Day 5	AM	5 miles easy s.s.r.
	PM	6 miles fast s.s.r.
Day 6		rest day.
Day 7	PM	15 miles medium s.s.r.

Week 3

Day 1	AM	5 miles easy s.s.r.
	PM	5 miles easy s.s.r.
Day 2	PM	8 miles medium s.s.r.
Day 3	AM	5 miles easy s.s.r.
	PM	8 miles medium s.s.r.
Day 4	PM	5 miles easy s.s.r.
Day 5	PM	12 miles medium s.s.r.
Day 6	AM	5 miles easy s.s.r.

The start of the London Marathon. Although the field of class runners at the front gets away quickly, it may take several minutes at walking rather than jogging pace before the remaining club athletes and fun runners get through the Greenwich Park gates to start

Day 7	AM	5 miles easy s.s.r.
	PM	8 x 1200m circuit (maintain previous times) maintain recovery jog.

Week 4

Day 1	AM	12 miles medium s.s.r.
	PM	4 miles easy s.s.r.
Day 2	PM	10 miles medium s.s.r.
Day 3	AM	5 miles easy s.s.r.
	PM	5 miles Fartlek.
Day 4	PM	8 miles easy s.s.r.
Day 5		rest day.
Day 6	AM	3 miles easy s.s.r.
Day 7		marathon race.

In addition, I would recommend 30 minutes of mobility exercises twice each week and 15-20 minutes of leg-strengthening exercises once or twice a week.

Marathon racing calls for a quite different approach to that adopted for shorter races although one principle should remain the same – your racing should reflect the fitness you have achieved in your training.

If you are at the top of the marathon tree then your racing tactics will be influenced to some extent by those adopted by your chief rivals. You race at a pace that is within your capabilities, but now and then may have to risk stepping up a gear in order to match the pace injected by one or other of your opponents. When this happens it is quite possible to go into a small oxygen debt which should be repaid quickly when the pace eases off again. This is where those occasional sessions when you exercised the lactic anaerobic system should stand you in good stead.

Some marathon runners are well known for their ability to 'push-it' up hills and when this happens you must make a quick decision – whether to go with their surge or whether to maintain your rhythm and close the gap when you get back on the flat.

If you are not yet of this elite calibre then I recommend that you use your races as exercises in pace judgement. Your long training runs should give you a pretty good indication of the sort of marathon time you may expect, so use this time as your target. Set intermediate target-times at 5, 10, 15, 20 and 25 miles and try to run relaxed whilst matching these times.

Going off too fast inevitably leads to moments of pain in any endurance event, but when it happens in a marathon the moments last for a mighty long time. So, going off too fast is usually the most common cause of a marathon runner not being able to stick to his pre-race schedule. I learned this from personal experience when during

This is among the toughest and most challenging marathons in the British Isles – the Snowdon Marathon. It is run on a hilly course

Here the Japanese runner Shigematsu runs in the Polytechnic Marathon. Japanese athletes have been at the forefront of marathon running

the Windsor to Chiswick Marathon in 1958, I set off too fast and this led to my aspirations in the event being abandoned once and for all. I had set off at a ridiculous pace for the first 10 miles, but felt good (don't we all?) but then gradually got slower and slower. The last straw came at about 25 miles when I looked to my left and realised that a woman was pushing a pram faster than I was running! I finished the race, said to myself, "Never again", and stuck to my words. So, level pace is important, relaxation is essential and keeping alert to what is going on around you is vital also.

Refreshments and diet

If refreshments need to be taken during a race, usually in hot and humid conditions, then you should try to take them without stopping so as not to interfere with your running rhythm. This can be done by using the special containers that have nozzles attached. You pick up the container, stick the nozzle in your mouth and squirt in the liquid by squeezing the body of the container – all this while you are still on the run. On these hot days, refreshments should be taken early in the race so that your body has sufficient time to assimilate the liquid.

You must find out which refreshment suits you personally and arrange for your containers to be clearly marked so that you can spot them as you draw level with the drinks table. The usual drinks are lime or orange juice, reinforced with glucose, i.e. liquids that are quickly assimilated and provide you with sugar. In warm weather you are going to lose body salts due to sweating and there are now many special marathon cocktails available that contain quantities of the vital minerals. Whatever you do, do not experiment with a new concoction during a race – always have a trial taste during a long training run. Cold sponges can be very refreshing, but once again should be used without any break in your running. Try to be a little careful with the distribution of the water in the sponge as the last thing you want when you are tired is a vest that is heavy by being saturated with liquid.

Some marathon runners use a special pre-race diet which has the objective of stimulating your body to store an abnormal amount of glycogen. The runner does a 20-25 miles training run seven days before a marathon race and this run has the effect of depleting the body's glycogen reserves. From then on until lunchtime on the Wednesday before a Saturday race, this glycogen reserve is kept at a deliberately low level by abstaining from carbohydrates and by eating a diet of exclusively fats and proteins. Imagine how your body is crying out for sugar which you are denying it. During this period training should be kept very light, i.e. easy steady-state runs of 5 or 6 miles.

After lunchtime on the Wednesday you switch to a heavily carbohydrate-enriched diet until the race-day and your body responds by storing up an enormously large reserve of glycogen. The glycogen level can rise to as much as three to four times its normal level and is there to be called upon once you pass the 20-mile mark. During the non-carbohydrate days you feel very weary and are usually bad-tempered but you must stick to your plan and put up with the rather tasteless and monotonous diet. Do not think that this diet is any substitute for regular and progressive training and remember its value is only during the closing stages of a race. The two women marathon runners whom I have coached have not used this diet, but instead they have stocked up heavily with carbohydrates in the two or three days immediately prior to a race. Tony Simmons tried it on one occasion and gave it up because he felt so awful during the non-carbohydrate days. However, he has persevered on other occasions and has been pleased with the results.

CHAPTER EIGHT

YOUNG ATHLETES

In 1973, shortly after Steve Ovett had won the European Junior 800m Championship in Duisberg I had a request from a West German sports magazine to write an article outlining Steve's training. I duly wrote the article, but had it rejected on the grounds that the editor thought that it would mislead his readers, because I had under-stated Steve's training. In fact, I had told the truth – he *was* only training five times a week at the time. The irony is that five years later I wrote another article for a different West German magazine and on this occasion the editor doubted the accuracy of the article as he did not believe that anyone could train so intensively! The lesson for young runners is to be able to accept that their training must develop gradually over a long period. You must not study the schedules given in Chapter 6 and say immediately, "That's for me".

You may be serious about your athletics aspirations at the age of 14 but must be clever enough to appreciate that for a few years it is unwise to expect your body to adapt to intensive training while your limbs and muscles are still growing and developing. The same physiological principles will apply to you as to older athletes, but the training loads are lighter and not so intense. Remember that in your early teens you are still not sure which event will eventually become your best and not knowing this means that it is too early to start heavily loading one aspect of your training. It is interesting to reflect that at the age of 16, Seb Coe looked as though he was heading towards the 3000m and 5000m events, whereas Steve Ovett at the same age was a schools champion at 400m.

Yearly gains in strength and physique will guarantee a certain amount of improvement and in addition your haemoglobin level is still rising during your teens which means that you are gradually improving your ability to take up oxygen from the air you breathe in. Haemoglobin levels tends to level off at about 18 years for girls and at about 20 for boys and as your main growth spurt usually finishes at approximately the same time, any future improvement is going to come about as a result of training. Many young athletes find that their performances improve quite well on fairly light training up to the ages of 18-20 years and it is hard to face up to the fact that from then on training must become progressively harder if they are to maintain improvement.

This difficult age sets a particular problem for girls, as these are the years when they start to menstruate and when they can also experience a considerable change in their physique. It is relatively common to see girls at the age of 16 who are ideally suited for endurance events by their slim physique, become, within a year, totally unsuited as a result of weight gained and changes to their figures and body shape. It is very important that during this stage, they eat a healthy balanced diet that contains plenty of fresh fruit and vegetables, and stay clear of too many carbohydrates and over-fatty foods.

Racing for young athletes

Frequent racing appeals to most young athletes but if you want to achieve reasonable results, you cannot go too heavy on your training. Whatever you do, do not jump to the conclusion that if a certain load of training is carried out by a top international athlete, then all you have to do is the same training and you will be just as good. Remember that it will have taken a first-class runner several years to achieve a particular training load and you must develop your own training build-up. I like to think that young runners are only training two or three times each week at the age of 14 and that it takes them four years before they are able to handle a schedule of six or seven sessions each week.

To those of you who are going to enjoy cross-country racing, I recommend three to four years of Winter training during which you gradually

Many young people, girls as well as boys, enjoy athletics and compete regularly against each other on the road, track and cross-country

increase the distance, frequency and speed of your steady-state run and also start developing the idea of high-quality aerobic sessions, i.e. repetitions round a grass or road circuit of distances varying from 1000m to 1500m. These repetitions should be performed at a fairly steady pace with only a short recovery period allowed.

During the track competition phase you should ensure that there is plenty of variety in your training for as yet you will still not be too sure which event is eventually going to become your speciality. The following charts show my ideas for this phase of your training. You will see that they cater for different age-groups and that they contain all the ingredients that go to make a well-balanced runner. These ingredients, which are denoted by code-letter are as follows:

A	Technique and speed
B	Aerobic capacity
C	Mobility
D	Strength
E	Anaerobic capacity

Suggested pre-track competition training for a 15-year-old 1500m runner. Train two days out of three – nine day cycle.

	Activity	Description of training
Day 1	A B	10min strides; 10min sprint drills. 10min rest; 5 miles fairly fast steady-state run.
Day 2	C E	15min mobility exercises; 10min rest. 2 sets of 5 x 400m at race-pace. 300m jog recovery between 400's, 4min walk/1 jog between sets.
Day 3		rest day.
Day 4	D B	15-20min strength activities; 10min rest. 7 miles medium steady-state run.
Day 5	A E	Strides and sprints as for Day 1; 10min rest. 3 x 800m at race-pace; 7-8 min walk/jog recovery between each.
Day 6		rest day.
Day 7	C B	15min mobility exercise; 10min rest. 4 x 1000m fairly steady with 1min jog recovery between each.
Day 8	D E	15-20min strength activities; 10min rest. 30min Fartlek.

Suggested pre-track competition training for a 16-year-old 1500m runner. Train three days out of four – 8-day cycle.

	Activity	Description of training
Day 1	A B	20min strides and sprint drills; 10min rest. 5 miles fast steady-state run.
Day 2	C E	20min mobility exercises; 10min rest. 2 sets of 6 x 300m at race-pace; 200m jog between 300's; 4min walk/jog between sets.
Day 3	D B	20min strength activities; 10min rest. 8 miles medium steady-state run.
Day 4		rest day.
Day 5	C E	20min mobility exercises; 10min rest. 4 x 800m at race-pace; 7-8 min jog/walk between each.
Day 6	A B	20min strides and sprints as for Day 1; 10min rest. 4 x 1200m fairly steady with 1min jog recovery between each.
Day 7	D E	20min strength activities. 10min rest. 30min Fartlek.
Day 8		rest day.

Suggested pre-track competition training for a 17-year-old 1500m runner. Train four days out of 5 – 10-Day cycle.

	Activity	Description of training
Day 1	A B	30min strides and sprint drills; 10min rest. 5 miles fast steady-state run.
Day 2	D B	25min strength activities. 10min rest. 8 miles medium steady-state run.
Day 3	C	20min mobility exercises; 10min rest.
Day 4	A B	30min strides and sprints as for Day 1; 10min rest. 5 x 1000m circuit fairly steady; 1min recovery jog between each.
Day 5		rest day.
Day 6	C E	20min mobility exercises; 10min rest. 600m fast (race-pace), 200m jog, 200m fast. Repeat 3 times with 7-8min jog/walk recovery between each.
Day 7	A B	30min strides and sprints; 10min rest. 5 miles fast steady-state run.
Day 8	D E	25min strength activities; 10min rest. 4 sets 3 x 200m fast; 30sec rest between each 200m; 4min walk recovery between sets.
Day 9	A B	30min strides and sprints; 10min rest. 8 miles medium steady-state run.
Day 10		rest day.

Sprint drills, mobility exercises and some strengthening exercises are illustrated in an earlier part of the book and I stress the importance of these activities to young athletes. A good running technique must be developed while you are young and I have already pointed out the contribution that strength and mobility make to an efficient style.

Of course, by concentrating heavily when you are young on one particular aspect of training you may well be able to make rapid advances in that specific area but I strongly recommend that you try to develop all the aspects of middle-distance training. I have known several young athletes who have concentrated solely on the aerobic side of their event when they were young and have discovered to their cost later on that they are let down by lack of speed or mobility. This is why I do not get carried away by such things as 'age-records', as I regard the test of a good runner as being the results that are achieved when he/she becomes serious. The early years are not an end in themselves; they are an apprenticeship to your senior career.

Remember that during the growing years your body needs energy for growth so make sure that you are not over-doing it by asking your body also to withstand the stress of intensive daily training. I also suspect that on occasions some young athletes have developed their muscular system in advance of the skeletal system as a result of heavy training. This can lead to various injuries, especially stress fractures of various parts of the legs and feet which are particularly common in young runners who are following heavy training programmes.

It is as though the engine of a motor-car has been developed well in advance of the chassis, with the consequent breakdown of several of the small mechanical parts.

I know that it is difficult at times to be patient and to develop gradually, believing that better results will come but, believe me, it is the best way. The heavens of middle-distance running are littered with examples of young athletes who shone brightly for a few brief years and then flickered and faded away.

CHAPTER NINE

LIFE AT THE TOP

Finally, let us look forward to the time when your efforts start to bring rewards and you make your debut on the international scene. What problems lie ahead? What obstacles have to be cleared? Are there pitfalls to be avoided? I have attended many major games and other international fixtures and have observed the way that various athletes face up to top-class athletics. I have sifted through these experiences and have chosen a few points that I consider worthy of discussion. They are not in any particular order but appear as they occurred to me.

First make the team

When you sit down and plan your racing and training programme for a year that includes one of the major Games such as the Olympic or World Championships, no doubt you will try to time your peak to coincide with the big event. In order to display that peak condition you have to make sure that you are in the team that goes to the Games, and thus you must also ensure that your fitness is sufficiently advanced to clinch your place. It is futile to be fantastically fit for a major event that takes place in September if you were not sufficiently fit to shine in the July trials.

At the Games

Having made the team and arrived at the Village, there will be several things that could surprise and maybe unsettle you.

The first thing will be that no other athlete really gives one jot about you. Everybody is so concerned with themselves and their own preparations that they have neither the time nor the inclination to bother with a newcomer. The team managers and coaches will try their best to help you but you have to remember that they will be responsible for several athletes and may not be able to give you all the attention you think you deserve. So you might feel a bit lonely and lost for a while until you come to grips with the reason for being there. You are there to produce your best form – so is everybody else – so try to become self-contained.

You will be lucky to have living conditions similar to home (sometimes they are better!) and it might seem inconvenient to share a room with another athlete, or to have very little privacy. Some athletes have totally different sleeping hours to others and you may hear ghetto-blasters late at night or games of dominoes at 4am. If these things start to affect your sleep, complain to the management – do not grin and bear it, and end up worn out. However, you will be lucky if you do not have at least one sleepless night, worrying about the forthcoming events but keep things like this in perspective. What is one sleepless night compared to hundreds of good solid snoozes?

At all major games you will find several restaurants, some of them open for 24 hours each day. Make sure that you do not over-eat and put on a few extra pounds, and try to avoid any large quantities of rich exotic food. Some of you will have favourite meals that you like to have before you compete. Do not let this become a fetish and cause you to worry if you cannot get your preferred dish. Make sure that you eat something suitable – something that is light, energy giving and easy to digest – and take the attitude that "missing my favourite meal isn't going to destroy hundreds of good training sessions."

You usually find yourself in the Games Village for a few days before your event begins so plan ahead to fill your time. Do not find that you have

Opposite: Steve Ovett savours his moment of triumph after winning the coveted gold medal in the 1980 Moscow Olympics. Ovett has remained one of the great British middle-distance runners

279

a few hours on your hands and say to yourself, "Well, I might as well go out for a run". There is a danger of being carried away by the opportunity to do extra training. Remember that you are really at the stage where you should be just marking time until your competition starts. Some athletes will go down to the training tracks intent on doing some easy strides and will get excited by the sight of several hundred spectators (many of them with cameras and stop-watches). Under these circumstances it is easy to get carried away and do a much faster session than planned.

Take the trouble to 'suss out' the stadium, the warm-up area, the reporting procedure and the 'waiting-room' so that these things are not strange to you on competition day. You usually have to finish your warm-up about 30 minutes before your race and spend the intervening time cooped up in a 'waiting-room' with your rivals. You really should rehearse this type of warm-up on some of your pre-games training sessions so that the long wait does not worry you. Try to stay relaxed in the 'waiting-room' – easier said than done, but some athletes get too tense and leave

Bislett Stadium in Oslo, Norway, is renowned throughout the athletics world for being a venue where new World Records in middle-distance events are set. But in spite of its illustrious reputation, it has only a small U-shaped cinder path for warming-up

their running behind in the call-up area. You usually get to know the starting list for your races 24 hours before the event. Assess the opposition – the team coach should be able to help here – but do not become obsessed with your rivals – you cannot make them any less fit. However, you are the master of your running – your job is to run up to or above your level of fitness.

Once you have been released to the stadium track, carry out one or two easy strides, then before the start of your race stand still for a few moments and remind yourself of the need to be mentally alert while you are running. I remember Steve Cram in the 1980 Olympic Games telling me that it took him two laps of his 1500m heat before he realised he was racing in the Games. Luckily his concentration returned and survived to make the final. He learnt a lot from that occasion

and I doubt if his concentration has wavered since then.

The European Circuit

The advent of Grand Prix and Permit meetings has meant that good-class runners can now compete all over Europe from early May to mid-September and if you have the iron constitution of Doina Melinte of Romania you could race in six different cities in 10 days. You are guaranteed good opposition if you can get invites for these meetings and of course they work wonders for your subvention fund. However, you need to be quite tough to last a week or two of this circuit and must be prepared to race well even though you feel shattered after travelling and very little sleep. The promoters are not so benevolent as to allow you the luxury of several nights in a hotel prior to a race in order to rest up. In most of the meetings you will find that the promoters have placed pace-makers in the middle-distance races, so expect to run fast on most occasions. Often you will find quite large fields on the starting line so you must be prepared to look after yourself in

Athletes competing in the Olympic Games stay usually in specially designed and built Games Villages. The atmosphere is friendly but the food and conditions are rarely homely. The buildings above were used for athletes attending the 1976 Montreal Olympic Games in Canada

what are frequently races of 'much bodily contact'. Plan your race-programmes carefully so that you do not take on too many races. The promoters quite rightly expect value for money, and poor performance can prejudice your chances of being asked to return next year, whereas a first-class run can bring invites from other promoters. Usually at these meetings you just have to report 40-50 minutes before your event to draw your numbers and after that you are left to fend for yourself in the warm-up area. Some of the warm-up facilities at these meets are not exactly Olympic Class. A typical example is the Bislett Stadium in Oslo where you are expected to warm-up on a sloping, U-shaped, 150m cinder path. Still it does not seem to affect people's performances in a Stadium that is famous for World Records in middle distance events.

Injuries and illnesses
These two subjects are each worthy of a complete book and plenty has been written about them elsewhere. My best advice to you is to establish contact with a good physiotherapist and a doctor who are sympathetic to your athletic aspirations so that you take positive action should you be ill or get injured.

Loss of form
Occasionally, for no apparent reason, your training begins to deteriorate and you start to produce poor performances. Years ago coaches and club officials would have said, "You're stale" and would have advised you that there was only one solution: "rest – have a break from running". This recommendation was always based on the premise that you had either trained too hard or raced too often, or both. I am sure that in many instances the diagnosis "You're stale" was much too conveniently simple and that other factors were really responsible for the loss of form. Here are a few things to look out for if you do feel that things are starting to slip away from you:

No challenge in training The danger signs are there when you start to dread training and on the way to the track say to yourself, "Oh no, not again". This can easily happen if you keep using the same track or continue pounding round the same circuit. I think that it is a good idea to change tracks occasionally, or try different circuits and new locations and then have a few days in totally different surroundings. I know the athletes I coach benefit from the weekends that we spend training on the beach and sand-dunes at Merthyr Mawr in South Wales even though it leaves them shattered for a day or two.

Too frequent racing (particularly at the same distance). The anticipation and excitement of competition releases adrenalin, which acts as a stimulant to the heart and you rely on this effect to give you that little bit extra in races. The effect is not there when you start feeling that "it's just another race", and this attitude can creep in if you constantly race the same event. I do feel that there is a limited number of times that you can draw on the "well of adrenalin" in order to provide inspiration, and maybe your body is telling you, "give me a break, I'm starting to run dry". You will see from the training schedules that I have specifically suggested racing at under and over your main event and these races will give you variety as well as producing a good training effort.

Insufficient sleep or rest In an earlier chapter I pointed out that your body needs time to recover from intensive training sessions, so unless you get plenty of rest you never really get over one session before you start another.

Frequent late nights (or early mornings) at discos may do wonders for your social image but will not win you medals. Feeling jaded and weary is quite different from the slightly tired "aching" feeling that is experienced by most runners when they are training regularly twice a day, but this feeling quickly disappears when you start warming-up for a race or a training session.

A poor or inadequate diet As a runner who trains regularly, your dietary requirements are totally different from the average person in the street who lives a fairly sedentary life. It is quite common for a runner to be using 4000 calories of energy so it is vital that his food intake matches this requirement. In addition, protein and iron are constantly being broken down in training and these food constituents must be replaced. By keeping a careful check on your weight you can see if there is any need to either increase or decrease your calorie intake. Once you are training regularly your weight should stay fairly constant. If you notice that you start losing weight then check that your intake is sufficient. Carrying extra weight is fatal for a middle-distance runner. You require more energy to drive an overweight body and the extra bulk also restricts your movements. An experienced coach or physiotherapist will soon tell you if you are overweight. They quickly develop a keen eye for detecting the extra pounds that accumulate – usually around the stomach, hips, backside and thighs.

It is important to check that your diet contains adequate quantities of carbohydrates, fats, proteins, vitamins and minerals and here are a few simple rules to follow:

1 Try to avoid those foods that only contribute calories (cakes, sweets, biscuits, etc) without also supplying proteins, vitamins and minerals.
2 Avoid foods that are too fatty. Fat is slow to digest and stays rather a long time in your stomach.
3 Eat plenty of fresh fruit and vegetables.
4 Ensure that there is plenty of protein in your diet – lean meat, poultry, fish, milk and cheese are good examples of protein-rich foods.
5 Check that your diet regularly contains such iron-rich foods as: liver, corned beef, sardines, raisins and haricot beans.

Several of the athletes I coach, Kirsty Wade and the Tooby twins are examples, are vegetarians (mainly because they do not like meat) and these athletes regularly check with dieticians to ensure that their diet is adequate.

A low haemoglobin level Haemoglobin is the substance in your blood that pulls out oxygen, and therefore a low level of haemoglobin can be a common cause of poor performance. The haemoglobin content of your blood is measured in grams per 100 millilitres and for the average male middle-distance runner the figure will be 15.8 grams. The average woman runner will have a figure of approximately 13.8 grams. Intense training results in the destruction of red cells which are normally replaced by a sound diet, but occasionally the iron metabolism is disturbed and there is a lowering of the red cell level. If you suspect that this may be your trouble, consult your doctor who will quickly arrange for you to have a haemoglobin test. If the test results in a figure significantly lower than those quoted then it is usual for the doctor to prescribe an iron supplement to the diet. Such a supplement should always be taken in consultation with a doctor or physiologist.

Stress On occasions you can be so stressed by outside pressures that you are unable to concentrate on training or racing. Problems associated with work, studies, finance and personal relationships for instance, can worry you so much that your general health can be affected let alone your athletic performance. If you are in such a position it would be asking for trouble to also expect to train intensively. Under these conditions your training should be kept to a minimum until your problems have eased and you can return to normal training. Easy running can take your mind off problems but if you are in a stressful situation it would be wrong to add more stress by expecting to concentrate on intensive training.

Still, it is not sufficient just to say, "I've got problems – I'll ease off training until they go away." You have to take sound action to solve your problems.

This section has outlined a few of the problems that you may come across when you are competing at a high level but it would be wrong of me to finish off in such a negative manner. By intelligent training and careful planning you have thrust your way into the international scene; enjoy it and savour it – you will have earned it. As you walk off the track after a good performance, think back to all those difficult training sessions and say to yourself, "This is what they were all in aid of – getting the best out of myself and enjoying the feelings that go with being a satisfied runner."

Bibliography

Books

BAAB: *Middle and Long Distance Running*
Cerutty, Percy: *How to Become a Champion*
Clarke, Ron: *The Lonely Breed* (Pelham Books)
Dyson, Geoffrey: *Mechanics of Athletics*
Dyson, Sandra, Etchells, Andy, Farrell, Mike, Milroy, Patrick, Rockall, Al, Stein, Sylvester, Temple, Cliff, Turnbull, Alison, Watson, Ray, Whiteson, Adrian, and Wilson, Harry:
The AAA Runner's Guide (Collins 1987, revised edition)
Elliott, Herb: *The Golden Mile* (Cassell & Co 1961)
Hemery, David: *Another Hurdle* (Heinemann 1976)
Holman, Ron, and Humphreys, John: *Focus on Middle Distance Running* (A & C Black 1985)
Horwill, Frank, Watts, Denis, and Wilson Harry: *The Complete Middle Distance Runner* (Stanley Paul 1972)
IAAF: *The IAAF Symposium on Middle and Long Distance Events*
Karpovitch, Peter: *Physiology of Muscular Activity (W.B. Saunders Co.)*
Ovett, Steve, and Rodda, John: *'Ovett'* (Collins Willow 1984)
Read, Dr Malcolm: *Sports Injuries* (Breslich & Foss 1984)
Schmolinsky, Gerhardt: *Track and Field Training in the GDR* (Distributed in the UK by Central Books, London)
Wilson, Harry: *Running Dialogue* (Stanley Paul 1982)
Wilt, Frank: *How They Train*

Magazines

Athletics Today (Lyon Street, Windsor Avenue, London SW19 2SE)
Athletics Weekly (342 High Street, Rochester, Kent ME1 1ED)
Runner's World (1400 Stierlin Road, Mountain View, California 94043)
Running Magazine (57-61 Mortimer Street, London W1N 7TD)

INDEX

All numerals in *italics* refer to photographs

A

B

C

USA
mazda
237
HOOSIER DOME

G

H

I

J

K

L

PEARL
16
ASSURANCE
PEARL
29
ASSURANCE
27
32
22
19

P

R

S

T

V

W

Y

Acknowledgements

The author and Publishers would like to extend their thanks to Johann Boakes and Josephine White who very kindly agreed to be photographed for the section on Technique (pages 24-35).

Picture credits

We would like to thank the following people and agencies for supplying pictures for reproduction in this book:

All Sport Photographic Ltd: pages 117 and 118
BBC Hulton Picture Library: page 51
Howard Payne: pages 64-65
Mark Shearman: cover and pages 5, 6, 8-9, 15, 16, 17, 18, 19, 20, 21, 22, 24, 25, 26, 28, 29, 30, 31, 34, 35, 43, 48, 49, 50, 51, 55, 57, 59, 60, 61, 62, 63, 66, 68, 69, 71, 74, 80, 82, 84, 86, 88, 91, 92, 94, 96, 98-99, 101, 102, 103, 105, 107, 108, 109, 111, 115 and 116